"Andy Lee digs deep into the rich origins of scripture to help readers nourish their faith-roots and grow into flourishing women of Christ. *Radiant Influence* connects Esther's story with our modern journey. I cannot recommend Lee's writing more highly *for such a time as this.*"

TINA YEAGER, author, speaker, life coach, *Flourish-Meant* podcast host, and *Inkspirations Online* publisher

"Humility, realness, and wisdom absolutely radiate off of her, just as they do from the pages of this powerful and relevant Bible study. Do yourself a favor; come close and listen in. God is speaking through Andy Lee, and you don't want to miss a word of it. "

HANNAH C. HALL, best-selling and award-winning author, blogger, and speaker

"I believe God loves questions because He uses conversation to build relationship with us. For this reason, along with many others, I celebrate how *Radiant Influence* beautifully encourages readers to explore the mysteries of God. Instead of avoiding hard questions or potentially confusing text, we dive in to engage with God through active and prayerful study. Andy's relatable stories easily prompt self-reflection and conversation as she guides readers to know God more in powerful and practical ways. "

JEN WEAVER, Ministry Coach, Author of *A Wife's Secret to Happiness*

"Even if you've never tried digging into archaeology, ancient history, or biblical languages before, with Andy as your guide, you'll find yourself enthralled, equipped, and growing. Andy's clever humor, sincere spirituality, and relatable stories draw you in and keep you engaged. She helps you step into familiar Bible stories and read them in new ways, finding fresh applications for your own walk with God. *Radiant Influence* is perfect for anyone seeking to deepen their own Bible study and would make a fantastic resource for small groups and book clubs!

ELIZABETH LAING THOMPSON, author of *All the Feels, When God Says, "Wait,"* *When God Says, "Go,"* and *When God Says, "No."*

"Andy Lee is a true woman of The Word! Having spent many years researching for understanding of hard biblical truths she brings invaluable wisdom that will transform your life for the better through the pages of her recently published book you are holding in your hands. *Radiant Influence* offers word wisdom we might otherwise overlook. Trust me when I say: Andy's influence will inspire you to pursue the heart of God – going deeper spiritually than you ever thought possible to transform your life for the better!"

LaTan Murphy, award-winning author of
Courageous Women of the Bible and co-host of *Past to Power* podcast.

"*Radiant Influence* is just like Purim, it's a feast. It offers the busy woman an opportunity to study the Bible but doesn't skimp on serving up the very best. Andy Lee skillfully includes cultural knowledge, word studies, and most importantly honors the Jewishness of the book of Esther. You may think you know Esther well, but this study packs a banquet of knowledge into bite-sized lessons. If you enjoy a little meat in your bible study, *Radiant Influence* will not disappoint."

Lauren Crews - author of *Strength of a Woman: Why You Are Proverbs 31*

Radiant Influence

HOW AN ORDINARY GIRL
CHANGED THE WORLD

A STUDY OF ESTHER

ANDY LEE

A BUSY WOMAN BIBLE STUDY

CR

ST JOSEPH, MISSOURI USA

RADIANT INFLUENCE: HOW AN ORDINARY GIRL CHANGED THE WORLD - A STUDY OF THE BOOK OF ESTHER

Copyright © 2021 Andy Lee

ISBN: 978-1-936501-58-8

For more information on Andy Lee, please visit WordsbyAndyLee.com

Editor: Debra L. Butterfield

Cover and Interior Designer: Tamara Clymer

Cover Art: ID 197154884 © Denys Kolisnychenko | Dreamstime.com

Printed in the United States of America.

To Lauren Lee Luce

You are a woman of radiant influence.
The Lord's love shines in your countenance,
and you are changing your world.

Contents

CONTENTS

Acknowledgments 9

The Why Behind the 5 11

Introduction 13

Week One

Day One - Convinced 17

Day Two - When Pain Paves the Way 21

Day Three - Generations of Faith 26

Day Four - Meet King Ahasuerus 30

Day Five - Meet Queen Vashti 34

Video Notes 39

Week Two

Day One - Ugly Pride 41

Day Two - A Different Kind of Law 46

Day Three - Remembered 50

Day Four - Purified 55

Day Five - No Longer Free 61

Video Notes 65

Week Three

Day One - Favored 67

Day Two - God's Favor 72

Day Three - Summoned by Name 76

Day Four - God's Compassion 81

Day Five - The Bride of Christ 85

Video Notes 89

Week Four

Day One - Accepted and Loved... 91

Day Two - Chosen... 96

Day Three - Delayed Rewards 100

Day Four - Persecuted for Faith 104

Day Five - Repentance..110

Video Notes 115

Week Five

Day One - Fasting and Trusting 117

Day Two - Getting Dressed 124

Day Three - Fight...129

Day Four - For Generations to Come...135

Day Five - Identity 140

Video Notes 145

Finally..147

Leaders Guide and Purim Parties..148

Endnotes..154

Bibliography..156

About the Author 157

ACKNOWLEDGMENTS

If you want to experience fully surrendering your timetable and dreams to God, be a writer. It's been five years since *The Ruth Bible Study: A 31 Day Journey to Hope and Promise* (AMG) and *A Mary Like Me: Flawed Yet Called* (Leafwood) were published. God had given me a double portion. Two books were published by different houses within two months after a seven year wait. I was elated. My juices were flowing, so I wrote a study on Esther and began to write proposals for other books, but nothing happened. God even opened a door to go back as an educator teaching sixth through twelfth grade ELA classes. There were days when I wondered if I would publish any more books. Don't they say that those who can't, teach? My friends, that is not true.

I had wondered why some authors didn't publish books more often, but then I became one of those authors. I now understand it takes time, persistence, and the right people in your life to encourage you and help you put your projects together. He's always been faithful to give me precious sisters to encourage my writing. Thank you to **Venus Schrader, Maureen Hayslett, Sandy Chambers, Kristin Eitland**, and my writing buddies of **Word Weavers Wilmington** to keep me going.

This time the Lord blessed me with the team at CrossRiver Media to publish this project. Thank you, **Debra Butterfield, Tamara Clymer**, and **DeeDee Lake,** for your excitement for *Radiant Influence* and your expertise and vision. I believe the Lord led me to you and your ministry to women. It's an honor to be on your team.

Finally, I'm so thankful for the man who swept me off my feet thirty years ago. Thank you, **Mike Lee,** for never thinking for one second my writing ministry was over. I love you.

From
Andy

THE WHY BEHIND THE 5

As I began to write *Radiant Influence,* God whispered, "Andy, you have too many questions." I knew He was right. (Of course, He's right!) In our culture of drive-thrus, Door-Dash, and text messages, most of us don't have time nor aptitude for long studies. Life isn't like it was twenty years ago when I first started doing Bible study as a desperate young mom. No Facebook or Instagram. I didn't have a computer yet! (Yes, I'm old.)

The Lord's whisper was followed by the number five…five questions, five days, five weeks. The Father is intentional in every detail, so I researched the meaning of the number five in Hebrew. Ya'll, it's so cool. The word is *chamesh* (khaw-maysh). Here are the meanings associated with five and the symbolism of the fifth letter of the Hebrew alphabet, the *Hey*:

> "*Chamesh [f.], chameeshah [m.] Power, strength, alertness (wake-up!), Torah, grace, service, gospel, fruitfulness, going forth, fast movement, anointed, prayers, and protection…Fifth Hebrew letter:* **Hey** *Numerical value of five. Pictographic meaning breath, air, spirit, femininity, and behold (to make known)…Five is indicative of being filled, prepared, and empowered to go forth on whatever mission YHWH has given one to do.*"[1]

I was blown away. Read it again. I know I'm a word nerd, but each meaning made me want to jump up and down. I could not think of anything that so perfectly defined everything I hoped my Bible studies would do. It is my prayer that every woman who participates in a *Busy Woman Bible Study* is *filled, prepared, and empowered to go forth on whatever mission YHWH has given her to do.*

Dear sister, I pray this format blesses you, encourages you, and draws you closer to the King of kings, our Radiant King. Now that we've got the "why five" behind us, it's time to learn the why behind this beloved story, and why we read our Bible.

It may surprise you.

andy

Start with God

INTRODUCTION

I wish you could see him. My faithful kitty Hank is lying next to my computer as I type. He's my buddy. He's pretty constant (for a cat). We need living beings in our life who are constant, people (and pets) we can depend on. Hank, my husband, and my BFFs are my constants. The Bible is too, so when I unearthed controversy in my research, it caused me to lose my breath for a moment. I had to regroup and dig further.

That's what happened when I began writing this study. I came upon a road bump concerning the authenticity of Esther. So, before we start this adventure, I want to take you back to the purpose of the Bible, because that's where I had to go.

Usually, we read the Bible to see what it says to us, but the Bible exists first and foremost to tell us about God. That's where we're going to start. With God. His goodness, kindness, and faithfulness. Close your eyes and take a deep breath. Let it out slowly. Spend a moment thanking him and worshiping before you read on.

CONTROVERSY

We begin with God himself because mystery and controversy hover over the book of Esther. Names and dates don't line up. It was not found in the Dead Sea Scrolls, which indicates the Qumran community, a revered holy Jewish sect, may not have accepted Esther as Scripture.[2] This community set themselves apart from the world to focus on God and the Torah. They were commended for their faith and sacrificial lifestyle.

I had to ask myself, "How do I write a Bible study on a book that some do not consider an actual event?" After much prayer, I found a solution. Rather than focusing on the details, I would focus on what the story teaches me about God Himself. Remember, that's who the Bible is about. Even if the historical facts aren't accurate, names misconstrued, and the story exaggerated in parts, an essential truth holds the narrative together. That truth is the goodness of God.

**The controversy of Esther's historical proof
does not change that.**

Despite the controversy, there are reasons to believe Esther did happen. One of those is the festival called Purim. This is the festival ordained by Esther to remind the Jewish people of God's salvation. An entire nation still celebrates this holiday, and the book of Esther is read aloud every year during Purim. Surely thousands of years of tradition prove its authenticity and relevance.

There is also proof that Jesus celebrated Purim. In the fifth chapter of John Jesus travelled to Jerusalem to celebrate a feast that fell on a Sabbath. The only feast that occurred on a Sabbath in the years of 25–35 C.E. was Purim.[3]

This is all I need to believe in the truth and relevance of Esther.

Why am I telling you about this debate when I believe that all the Bible was inspired by God? **I think it's important to study a scripture from all angles.** It's healthy to question and recognize other's beliefs. This makes us do our homework. It makes our conviction stronger. I'm the last person who will jump into debate, but if we don't question, and we don't study beyond what we've always been taught, our faith will be static.

Also, **it's necessary to study outside our Christian perspective and study Jewish commentary and rabbinical interpretation.** Analyzing these references help us better understand historical and literary context. Don't forget we've been grafted in, adopted into their family.

> If some of the branches have been broken off, and you, though a wild olive shoot, have been grafted in among the others and now share in the nourishing sap from the olive root, do not consider yourself to be superior to those other branches. If you do, consider this: You do not support the root, but the root supports you. You will say then, "Branches were broken off so that I could be grafted in." Granted. But they were broken off because of unbelief, and you stand by faith. Do not be arrogant, but tremble. For if God did not spare the natural branches, he will not spare you either.

> Consider therefore the kindness and sternness of God: sternness to those who fell, but kindness to you, provided that you continue in his kindness. Otherwise, you also will be cut off. And if they do not persist in unbelief, they will be grafted in, for God is able to graft them in again (Romans 11: 17–23 NIV).

God loves His *first* chosen people. Please don't forget that the story of Esther is theirs. Though thousands of years separate us from Esther, God's saving arm and Presence will never change, nor His words. **What God did for Esther and her people, He has and will do for you.** Though we need to know the details, we can't get lost in debates or questions. Just look for everything this wonderful story tells you about God. Remember to ask yourself that question first, then apply the truth to your life. When we study this way, **His spirit, His truth, and radiant influence will change us, which in turn will change our world.**

Breathe deep.

Let's begin.

Week One

DAY 1
CONVINCED

I know we want to jump into the book of Esther, but first, I want to set the stage of our study on influence. The themes we will come back to time and time again are purpose, presence, and identity.

Surely, none of us would be where we are today without the people of faith whom the Lord deposited into our lives and hearts. God faithfully places people along our path who live by faith and not by sight. Their faith is contagious. It draws us in and makes us hungry to know God.

As we study Esther, we'll see the influence of Mordecai, her adoptive father. Most of the time we focus on Esther, but if it hadn't been for Mordecai, the ending would not have been the same.

Those people in my life whose faith influenced mine include those who at times struggled to believe when life got hard. It wasn't their perfect walk that drew me near. Sometimes it was their struggle that forced me to do my own reckoning of faith, to get on my knees, search deep the scriptures, and find truth for myself.

The relationships that affected my trust in God include three women who I know are watching from above. They are three generations of faith lived out through disease and death. Though my grandmother, mother, and sister may have questioned why, they never questioned the reality or goodness of God. And neither will I.

> Most of the time we focus on Esther, but if it hadn't been for Mordecai, the ending would not have been the same.

〰 DAILY READING

Our study's foundational scripture:

"But as for you, continue in what you have learned and have become convinced *of, because you know those from whom you learned it, and how from infancy you have known the*

Holy Scriptures, which are able to make you wise for salvation through faith in Christ Jesus. All Scripture is God-breathed and is useful for teaching, rebuking, correcting and training in righteousness, so that the servant of God may be thoroughly equipped for every good work" (2 Timothy 3:14–17 NIV emphasis mine).

When Paul wrote that all Scripture is "God-breathed," the Scripture Timothy had at the time was the Old Testament.

Sidenote: Have you ever considered that when Paul wrote that all Scripture is "God-breathed," the Scripture Timothy had at the time was the Old Testament? The New Testament had not been collected, some not even written. Therefore, we should study the Old Testament, too. Anyway, let's dig in.

This admonition was Paul's final instruction to Timothy. What reason does Paul give Timothy to continue in his conviction or assurance of Scripture's truth?

List the people in your life whose faith helps you believe in the truth of the Bible.

Choose one of those names and write down how her life encourages your faith.

According to this passage, for what purpose is every scripture God-breathed?

Reread verse 14. Are you convinced of the truth of the Bible even if Esther is not a historical story? Why or why not?

✎ JOURNAL

Write a prayer asking God to give you a deeper revelation and understanding of Him and a stronger conviction of your faith as you study Esther.

💡 WORD STUDY

The word *convinced* was translated from *Pistoo* (pis-to'-o.) It's only found in this verse in the entire Bible, which I think is really interesting. The root of this word is *Pistos.*

CONVINCED - Greek Strong's Number 4103

πιστός pistós, *pis-tos'; objectively, trustworthy; subjectively, trustful:—believe(-ing, -r), faithful(-ly), sure, true.*

Circle the word *faithful.*

FAITH JOURNAL

Purchase a notebook or journal and keep track of the ways you witness God's faithfulness. From the changing of season to His provision, God's faithfulness surrounds us every day. Keeping a journal opens our eyes and reminds us of these treasures.

CHANGE YOUR WORLD

We have lost the art of writing letters, but they are special gifts. Write and mail a letter to one of the people whose faith encouraged yours, thanking her for the influence she had on your life.

Assurance and conviction cultivate faithfulness. **I know faithfulness comes easier when we have no doubts, but I've experienced that clinging to my faith, even in seasons of doubt, strengthens it.**

Faithfulness, however, is a two-way street. Though it seems our conviction depends on us, the One whom we have been called to believe in is faithful. *He* is faithful. This is why we can be confident in our convictions.

✋ HOLD HIS HAND

"Father, You are faithful. Thank You for the faithful believers You place in my life to help me believe. Lord, strengthen my faith. I want to be *pistoo* (pis-to'-o.) I want to be that faithful, gut-wrenching woman of faith for others. I want my *pistoo* (pis-to'-o) to change the world. Use me. Amen."

☕ QUESTION FOR GROUP DISCUSSION

How does our ability to perceive God's faithfulness affect our conviction? How can being convinced affect our faithfulness to God? Share an example from your life.

WHEN PAIN PAVES THE WAY

I recently read *The Hiding Place* by Corrie Ten Boom. If you haven't watched the movie or read the story, I recommend doing so, but I must warn you, it's sad. Her family owned a small clock and watch shop in Haarlem, Netherlands, during World War II. Their shop became an intricate part of the underground effort to help Jews, and they housed and hid Jews who had nowhere to go. Though Christians, they were imprisoned in German concentration camps when they were caught.

After months of internment, Betsie and Corrie were moved to one of the harshest camps. In their new barracks, Corrie discovered their mattresses were riddled with fleas. She cried out to Betsy, and they began to pray. Betsie, who always found good in everything told Corrie they should give God thanks. Corrie struggled with this prayer, but weeks later they realized the blessing in disguise. Because of the fleas, guards refused to enter the infested building. With no guards, the sisters were able to hold worship services every night. Read Corrie's description of the worship:

Faith does not prevent suffering, but faith provides strength to walk through doors of great purpose often opened by sorrow and strife.

> *"They were services like no others, these times in Barracks 28. A single meeting night might include a recital of the Magnificat in Latin by a group of Roman Catholics, a whispered hymn by some Lutherans, and a sotto-voce chant by Eastern Orthodox women. With each moment the crowd around us would swell, packing the nearby platforms...At last either Betsie or I would open the Bible. Because only Hollanders could understand the Dutch text we would translate aloud in German. And then we would hear the life-giving words passed back along the aisles in French, Polish, Russian, Czech, back to Dutch. They were little previews of heaven, these evenings beneath the light bulb...in the darkness God's truth shines most clear."[4]*

We never want to go through hard things. We spend most our life trying to be comfortable and happy. But often our difficulties and pain become places of preparation. Faith does not prevent suffering, but faith provides strength to walk through doors of great purpose often opened by sorrow and strife.

DAILY READING

Read Esther 2:5–7

What did you learn about Esther in this passage?

How could being an orphan affect Hadassah's character? (Hadassah is Esther's Hebrew name.)

EXTRA!

According to David Guzik of *The Enduring Word* commentary, the meaning of Hadassah, which is "myrtle," holds great significance. He writes, "In prophetic symbolism the myrtle would replace the briars and thorns of the desert, so depicting the Lord's forgiveness and acceptance of his people. (Isaiah 41:19; 55:13; cf. Zechariah 1:8)"[5]

I love how this meaning relates to the destiny she would fulfill for her people. Okay, let's keep going.

Could her past prepare her for what was to come? How?

As I asked this question to my Esther group—women I've met with for a year—it was so interesting to hear their answers. As they shared their thoughts, I could see how their past colored their interpretation. One who was raised by her grandparents said, "Oh, I think she would've tried really hard to please her elders and do everything right." Another lady who was very shy as a child added her thoughts, "I think losing your parents would make you very quiet and timid." While one more member of my group shared, "I think this would force her to be bold and take authority in situations because she had to."

In each of their answers I saw each woman—her past, her personality. And that, my friends, is how we read our Bibles. We read and interpret Scripture with our filters. Our experiences, wounds, and blessings. The educated word for this way of reading Scripture is *hermeneutical biases*. We all have them. They aren't bad, but we need to be aware.

It's difficult to judge Esther's character until we read the rest of the story. Actions speak louder than words, and Esther's (Hadassah's) actions speak volumes. But before we get ahead of ourselves, this lesson has taught us about two aspects of her life that molded her: She was an adopted orphan and a Jew living in a foreign land.

Now let's look at Mordecai. Look back at Esther 2:5–7 again.

What did you learn about Mordecai in this passage?

What does this passage tell you about God?

✒ JOURNAL

When I was a little girl, my right foot wasn't normal. I don't think they identified the problem as a club foot, but it was very close to that condition. Braces and two surgeries helped. You'd never know my handicap by looking at me now. But even though my foot looks okay, and I walk fairly normal, my small handicap formed and shaped me. I think it made me kinder, more understanding, and sensitive to other's needs. What past hurt, handicap, or pain has shaped your personality?

💡 WORD STUDY

Read verses 5–6 in the ESV version and write down how many times the author uses the words "carried away."

Now there was a Jew in Susa the citadel whose name was Mordecai, the son of Jair, son of Shimei, son of Kish, a Benjaminite, ⁶who had been carried away from Jerusalem among the captives carried away with Jeconiah king of Judah, whom Nebuchadnezzar king of Babylon had carried away. - Esther 2:5–6 ESV

The Hebrew word translated as "carried away" is the word *galah*, gaw-law'. This word describes how the exiles were taken. It implies disgrace. Captives were usually stripped and paraded through the cities.

CARRIED AWAY - Hebrew Strong's Number H1540

הלָגַּ **gâlâh,** *gaw-law'; a primitive root; to denude (especially in a disgraceful sense); by implication, to exile (captives being usually stripped); figuratively, to reveal:— advertise, appear, bewray, bring, (carry, lead, go) captive (into captivity), depart, disclose, discover, exile, be gone, open, × plainly, publish, remove, reveal, × shamelessly, shew, × surely, tell, uncover.*

The repetition of words was a literary device used in Hebrew literature. It was used to make a point or help with memory. I believe the author of Esther is making a point here. The Jews have been hated and discriminated against for a long time. They'd been humiliated, shamed, and treated unfairly.

We cannot forget, the greatest Jew who suffered *galah* was God's Son. This truth became tangible to Corrie Ten-Boom. Every week the female prisoners were forced to strip and parade naked in front of the male guards as the they lined up to take a shower.

The thought of Christ's shame flashed through Corrie's mind as she walked behind her thin, sickly sister. At that moment she realized Jesus hung naked on the Cross. She whispered, "Betsie, they took *His* clothes too."

Betsie replied, "Oh, Corrie, And I never thanked Him…"[6]

"What shall we say in response to this? If God is for us, who can be against us?"

ROMANS 8:31–32

🖐 HOLD HIS HAND

"Dear Jesus, You suffered so much for me. Thank You. Thank You for climbing upon the Cross, *galah* (gaw-law') for the world to see. It breaks my heart. Lord, take my broken pieces, my shame, and my wounds, and make me a light in dark places."

☕ QUESTION FOR GROUP DISCUSSION

Read Matthew 27:27–31 and discuss what the soldiers did to Jesus. What does this scene tell you about the goodness of God?

GENERATIONS OF FAITH

Let's jump right in today. You read this yesterday, but you might have slept since then, so let's read it again to refresh our memories. Today, we are focusing on Mordecai's family line.

✍ DAILY READING

Read Esther 2:5–6

According to verse 6, what family line is Mordecai from? Who were the men in his family?

Just to clear up confusion...Bible scholars do not believe Mordecai was "carried away from Jerusalem" but rather his ancestor, Kish. Mordecai would be over one hundred years old during this story if he'd been in the exile, and scholars do not think that probable.[7]

To bring further clarity, Mordecai's heritage included these great men from the tribe of Benjamin, but the timelines don't add up for them to actually be father, grandfather, and great-grandfather. Instead of the exact generational flow, Hebrew writers often use prominent family names to reveal a powerful genealogy.[8] Though this seems trivial, it's something to keep in mind when reading other Bible stories and passages that involve genealogies. The writers always focus on the influential names.

How does the author describe Mordecai in Esther 2:5a (before the naming of his family)?

The name "Jew" was the name given to the people who came out of the land of Judah during the Babylonian exile. So, even though Mordecai's blood line flowed down through the tribe of Benjamin, all exiles from Judah were called Jews even if they were not from the line of Judah. Let's learn a little bit about Mordecai's ancestors Jair, Shimei, and Kish.

Read 2 Samuel 16:5–14. Who curses David and why?

Why does David stop his men from killing this man who curses him?

This may seem confusing. We know David as God's anointed, the man after God's own heart. So, when we read about Shimei cursing David, we automatically think of him as the bad guy. But we must remember that before King Saul lost his favor with God, he, too, was God's anointed. Shimei acted faithfully out of loyalty for his king and God. David would not allow his men to kill him because David said Shimei was doing what God told him to do. As we study further into this story, we will see those strong, loyal, faith-filled, and brave character traits in Mordecai.

What do Shimei's actions tell you about this family?

JOURNAL

Identity is huge. Though it's nice when people recognize us, it's more important to be secure in our own knowledge of who we are. The Jews knew they were God's people. Jesus knew he was the Messiah, the Son of God. When a person or group of people is secure in their identity, they can fulfill their purpose. Who are you? What's your identity? Don't give the answer you think is right; really look inside and write down what makes you, you. We'll visit this question again throughout the study.

IDENTITY

Read all of Psalm 139 today, making it your own. Copy the verses that speak to you in your Faithfulness Journal.

HISTORY

History books tell us that Jerusalem fell to Nebuchadnezzar, a Babylonian king, almost a century before Esther (Hadassah) became a queen. During his reign, Nebuchadnezzar ordered three deportations of the people of Judah. They were taken into captivity and exiled into Babylon, **present day Iraq.** Not all Jews were exiled. Some fled to surrounding countries while others stayed in Jerusalem. The Jewish nation was no longer autonomous. They were ruled by Babylon and dispersed throughout the world. This was known as the Jewish Diaspora.

My momma always told me life is like a teeter-totter—you can't stay at the top forever because the person on the other end has to go up. And so it was with Nebuchadnezzar's kingdom. The once great Babylonian nation fell to the Persians, **modern day Iran.** This was a good thing for the Jews because King Cyrus opened the doors for the Jews to go home if they desired—he encouraged them to return to Jerusalem and rebuild their Temple.

However, not everyone moved back home. Years had passed; they were settled. It isn't difficult to imagine the reasons why a Jewish family chose not to move back. The curtains were hung, pictures on the walls. The kids had new friends. It was costly to return. And for many of them, the last look at Jerusalem was one of total devastation. Their homes burned. The Temple destroyed. There was nothing for them to go back home to. I'm sure many felt stuck despite their new freedom. Jerusalem offered no security. With the wall destroyed, a move home would be dangerous and risky even though hatred for Jews made living anywhere menacing.

Six decades span the fall of Babylon and Hadassah's crown, so she must have been born years after the battles, and though we still don't know what orphaned this baby girl, we can be sure that she was born into a battle-weary family. Sojourners in a foreign land making the best of what they had. Desperately holding onto their faith and identity.

✋ HOLD HIS HAND

"Father, I can't imagine living during Esther's time. Forgive me when I'm not thankful for the freedom I have. Lord, I pray for the Jewish nation and the hatred and discrimination they've faced throughout history. Is there any way I can help turn the tide? Give me the confidence and strength of Mordecai's family. In Jesus's name I pray. Amen."

☕ QUESTION FOR GROUP DISCUSSION

Have you been taught that the Jews are bad? Discrimination against the Jews started before Jesus and continues today. Why do you think God's people, the Jewish people, have been hated and discriminated against for so long?

MEET KING AHASUERUS

Generous. Eccentric. Gluttonous. Extravagant. Those words describe King Xerxes. Xerxes was the Greek name for the Persian King Ahasuerus (his Hebrew name). He ruled from 486 to 465 B.C.[9] Xerxes is definitely the easiest name to remember and pronounce. But let's use his Hebrew name since that is his name in the Hebrew scrolls, Ahasuerus (akh-ash-rosh'). This is the official STRONG'S entry for the name of this eccentric king whose name fits his title.

> שׁוֹרֵשַׁחֲא **ʾĂchashvêrôwsh,** *akh-ash-vay-rosh'; or (shortened)* שׁרֵשַׁחֲא *'Achashrôsh (Esther 10:1); of Persian origin; Achashvero-sh (i.e. Ahasuerus or Artaxerxes, but in this case Xerxes), the title (rather than name) of a Persian king:—Ahasuerus.*

I might just stick with King A. My Oklahoma accent has trouble with foreign names.

King A. was a product of his culture. Persians were known for their drinking and elaborate parties. In fact, officials drank when making important decisions because they believed intoxication ushered them closer to the spiritual world's wisdom. According to Touraj Daryaee in his article about the history of drinking in Iran:

"The fifth century BCE historian Herodotus claimed not only that the Persians were very fond of wine, but that they routinely made important decisions while drunk on it. According to Herodotus, the day after such a drunken deliberation, the Persians would reconsider their decision and if they still approved, adopt it."[10]

According to Esther, however, King Ahasuerus did not take such liberality in reversing decisions. He declared that once his signet ring touched a proclamation, it could not be changed.

Several commentaries portrayed King Ahasuerus and all the characters of this story as one dimensional. But digging into the Hebrew text and taking time to consider each scene, rather than reading quickly, reveals the layers of each person. I want more than the Veggie Tale version. I think you do, too.

DAILY READING

Read Esther 1:1–4

Who was invited to the feast that lasted one hundred and eighty days?

Why would a king do this?

Why would the celebration last so long?

Read Esther 1:5–6. Who were invited to the seven-day feast and where was it held?

Describe the colors and design of the gardens.

I think it sounds beautiful. I would pin a picture on my Pinterest board if someone would've had a camera that day. The colors were deep and royal; the scarves flowing in the wind, and the mosaic floor a myriad of color under sandaled feet. Though the common folk couldn't enter the palace, he brought the palace out to them. I like that about him.

King A. seemed a gluttonous, drunk party animal, but at least he wasn't a stingy one. If indeed his feast for the officials lasted one hundred and eighty days and the feast for everyone "both great and small" for an entire week, it can be said that he was a generous king. We'll see his generosity again later in the story.

💡 WORD STUDY

One word in the Hebrew text reveals a good side to the king:

> *"Drinks were served in golden vessels of different kinds, and the royal wine was lavished according to the <u>bounty</u> of the king"* (Esther 1:7 ESV).

"Bounty" was translated from the word *yad* (yawd). I love the meaning of this word.

BOUNTY - Hebrew Strong's H3027

יָד **yâd,** *yawd; a primitive word; a hand (the open one [indicating power, means, direction, etc.], in distinction from 3709, the* *closed one); used (as noun, adverb, etc.) in a great variety of applications, both literally and figuratively…*

The open hand of the king was a powerful one, yet his open hand also revealed his generosity as opposed to a closed hand.

✎ JOURNAL

Read James 1:5. God is a generous King. Write down the blessings your open-handed King has given to you, to the church, and to the world. Thank Him.

✋ HOLD HIS HAND

"Dear God, thank You for being an 'open handed' God, a God of *yad* (yawd.) All that You have is mine. Help me step into that celebration every day. Make my heart glad. Thank You for favor, forgiveness, and joyful spirit. Amen."

☕ QUESTION FOR GROUP DISCUSSION

Do you struggle with generosity whether giving or receiving? Why?

GENEROSITY

"Praise be to God and Father of our Lord Jesus Christ, who has blessed us in the heavenly realms with every spiritual blessing in Christ."

EPHESIANS 1:3 NIV

DAY 5
MEET QUEEN VASHTI

On March 2, 1955, in Montgomery, Alabama, a fifteen-year old girl climbed aboard a city bus and sat with her friends in the rows designated for people with her skin color. As the bus filled, a white woman needed a place to sit, but her section was full. The bus driver insisted that the young girls sitting in their row next to the white section move in order for the woman to have a seat.

Claudette Colvin's friends got up and walked to the back, but Claudette would not budge. Though there was now room for the woman to sit next to the defiant, brave girl, the woman refused because Jim Crow laws made it illegal for blacks and whites to sit next to one another. According to the laws, blacks should always sit behind whites.

Colvin was removed from the bus by police and taken to jail. Her friends told her mother what happened, and her mother and pastor came to the jail to pay for her bail. Her pastor told her, "I'm so proud of you. Everyone prays for freedom…But you're different — you want your answer the next morning. And I think you just brought the revolution to Montgomery."[11]

Claudette's story, eclipsed by the renowned Rosa Parks, is not well known, but her actions planted a seed. On that day in 1955, a fifteen-year-old girl's bravery sparked preparations for a bus boycott that would be led nine months later by a pastor named Dr. Martin Luther King, Jr. that would change the world.[12]

⟋ DAILY READING

Read Esther 1:9

What did Queen Vashti do? For whom was her feast? And where was it held?

It's important to understand the culture as we read this story and make our inferences. According to commentary in The Jewish Study Bible, the wives of Persian nobility did not attend the male drinking parties. To do so was considered licentious. The only women at those parties were those who danced for the men.[13] Yep, we know what that means. Those events were like one big bachelor party. I wouldn't have wanted to attend either.

Why did Vashti hold her own party considering the commentary above?

Read Esther 1:10–12 What day was it? How is the king described?

Notice the different translations:

> *"On the seventh day, when the heart of the king was <u>merry</u> with wine…" ESV*

> *"On the seventh day, when King Xerxes was <u>in high spirits</u> from wine…" NIV*

When translations differ, that's my cue to do some digging.

💡 WORD STUDY

The Hebrew word translated to "merry" and "in high spirits" is *towb* (tove.) Generally, this word is translated as "good."

GOOD - Hebrew Strong's Number H2896

בֹוט **ṭôwb,** *tobe; from H2895; good (as an adjective) in the widest sense; used likewise as a noun, both in the masculine and the feminine, the singular and the plural (good, a good or good thing, a good man or woman; the good, goods or good things, good men or women), also as an adverb (well):—beautiful, best, better, bountiful, cheerful, at ease, × fair (word), (be in) favour, fine, glad, good (deed, -lier, -liest, -ly, -ness, -s), graciously, joyful, kindly, kindness, liketh (best), loving, merry, × most, pleasant, pleaseth, pleasure, precious, prosperity, ready, sweet, wealth, welfare, (be) well(-favoured).*

In contrast, the Hebrew word for *intoxicated* is the word *shathah* (shaw-thaw').

DRUNK - Hebrew Strong's Number H8354

הָתָשׁ **shâthâh,** *shaw-thaw'; a primitive root; to imbibe (literally or figuratively):—× assuredly, banquet, × certainly, drink(-er, -ing), drunk (× -ard), surely. (Intensive proposition of H8248.)*

Why would the author use the word *towb* to describe the king rather than *shathah*?

Perhaps the author chooses this word to demonstrate the sharp contrast, quick change of the king's personality after Vashti refuses his command. Perhaps he isn't drunk but simply "feeling good"—not intoxicated beyond reason. Why would this be important? Does this affect the story or your view of the king?

Read Esther 1:10–12 again. What did the king want Vashti to do and why?

Does this sound bad to you? Why do you think she refused? Two scenarios come to my mind explaining her refusal. One is that only "dancing women" attended those male parties as entertainment. Perhaps Vashti felt this was below her dignity or secondly, maybe she felt he was treating her as one of his trophies. He had just spent an entire half of the year showing off his kingdom. I've read several sources that theorize the king was commanding Vashti to wear nothing but her crown. Here's one:

> *"The refusal of Vashti to obey an order which required her to make an indecent exposure of herself before a company of drunk revellers, was becoming both the modesty of her sex and her rank as queen; for, according to the Persian customs, the queen, even more than the wives of other men, was secluded from the public gaze."*[14]

If the king had, in fact, commanded her to flaunt her naked body in front of the other men, that would definitely explain her refusal in my mind. But we have no *definite* reason that proves Vashti's decision. We only know she refused the order and faced the consequences for rejecting the king in front of those he was trying to impress. Surely if his wife could refuse him, others would too.

Vashti's role in Esther is short. We don't linger on her character for long or the cause for her dethronement, and the Bible is not clear about her fate. The *Veggie Tales* version banishes her, but other tales have her beheaded. Whether she lost her life or not, we don't know. We do know, however, she is no longer in the story because of her morals or at least her strength, and this opens a need for a new queen. It happens all the time. Tragic, unfair events are used for good (*towb*). I hope Vashti lived to see what happened as a result of her dethronement. Maybe knowing that her rejection of the king's command wasn't good for her but eventually for a nation gave her comfort.

JOURNAL

Write down a time something unfair happened to you or someone close to you that turned out to help another situation.

HOLD HIS HAND

"Father, this is a hard lesson. It doesn't seem fair, but I know it opened up the door for Esther to walk in and save her people. Help me live my life always looking for the *towb* (tove.) I know you work all things out for the good of those who love you. Thank you, Lord. Amen."

"And we know that in all things God works for the good of those who love him, who have been called according to his purpose" (Romans 8: 28 NIV).

QUESTION FOR GROUP DISCUSSION

Share your answer to the journal question.

WEEK ONE VIDEO NOTES

Week Two

DAY 1
UGLY PRIDE

At the sound of the knock, I ran to the door. I thought my son had forgotten something. But someone else stood at my door. The nicely dressed older woman, prepared to turn me into a Jehovah Witness, startled as I opened the door. Did I scare her?

I'd been very busy that morning cutting up orange slices for my son's lacrosse team. Though I'd been up for hours writing a blog post, preparing breakfasts, and snacks for the team, I'd not taken time to dress or brush my hair. So, there I stood in my pink fluffy robe with a messy head of hair at 9:30 in the morning. When I dared to open the door, I was thinking it was an hour earlier, and I could justify my robe, but as soon as I saw her face, I remembered it was later. There I stood incredibly busy but seemingly a late sleeper.

I knew what she was selling. She was worried about my salvation—probably even more now that I'd opened the door, standing in my robe late in the day. But before she could get very far into her script, I told her I loved Jesus and didn't need her material.

"Keep it," I told her as nicely as possible.

I grabbed her hand and asked her name.

"Elaine," she smiled.

"I'm Andy," I replied. "Thank you for coming by. You'll be in my prayers."

Her eyes danced as she took my hand and thanked me. "Your hands are so warm!"

"I've been working in the kitchen." I explained—thankful for the opportunity to let her know I wasn't lazy.

Why do I care so much about what other people think? That very same morning this lesson continued. The Lord was on a roll.

Remember those snacks I'd been busy preparing? To save time, I had allowed my son to drive our van to school with the snacks. I had given him specific orders to put the bottles of waters and snacks on the bus so the team would have them on the way to the game. I had planned to walk over to the school to pick up the van and drive to the game later. It was a perfect plan, but when I climbed into the driver's seat all my hard work was still inside my van. Andrew had not placed the snacks and waters on the bus.

I was tired. I'd worked hard all morning to have those snacks ready before the team left, but my son hadn't done as I asked. What did the coach think of me when there were no snacks on the bus? I burned within. Yes, burned. In a split second I was angry over a trivial matter. I started the van, put it into drive, and tried to trust my son had a good reason for his disobedience. Suddenly I remembered King A. and how he quickly went from a king with a "happy" or "good" heart to an angry one, and I could relate. But even worse, I knew my anger rose from pride. I was concerned that it appeared I hadn't done my job.

My actions would not be as severe as the king's were to Vashti, but my son would know my frustration. Thankfully, I had two hours to cool down and settle my thoughts before I reached the game. Andrew also had time to explain his actions via text messages. My anger subsided and all turned out well. The team ate their oranges at half-time, and the chips and water were placed on the bus for the drive home.

As I climbed into bed that night the Lord whispered, "Your day would've been less stressful if your pride hadn't been present."

⤳ DAILY READING

Read Esther 1:12. **How does your Bible translation describe the king?**

The ESV writes: "At this the king became enraged, and his anger burned within him."

☀ WORD STUDY

ENRAGED - Hebrew Strong's Number 7107

קָצַף **qâtsaph,** *kaw-tsaf'; a primitive root; to crack off, i.e. (figuratively) burst out in rage:—(be) anger(-ry), displease, fret self, (provoke to) wrath (come), be wroth.*

This word was indicative of anger that rose when a servant didn't do his job. The king was not the only biblical character who lost his temper like this. The same word is found describing pharaoh when he imprisoned the butcher and baker, and Moses when the Israelites did not follow the instructions about mana. In most instances the anger was justified, but not always.

Can you relate to the king's anger? Was your anger justified?

Read Esther 1:13,14. From whom did the king seek counsel and why?

I think this is important and overlooked as we read this familiar story. King A. did not make this decision on his own, nor did he go to his best buddies for counsel. The scripture states he received advice from the wise men who knew the law. Their decision was based on what happened according to law when someone defied the king.

According to Esther 1:15–18 who gave the verdict about Vashti and whom did he say she wronged beside King Ahasuerus? Why?

What is the solution suggested in Esther 1:19? What made this decision final, unable to be repealed?

The decree would be proclaimed to all the provinces in the kingdom through letters sent in every language of the people. At first glance, it doesn't seem like a big deal for this proclamation to be sent out in different languages. But a closer look at history reveals the uniqueness of this distribution and the reasoning behind it.

According to The Jewish Study Bible, normally, laws and messages were distributed in Aramaic, the language of the empire, and then translated for each village according to their language.[1] But in order to assure each man maintained authority in his home, the proclamation was written in many different languages *so that every husband could readily understand the message and report the contents to his wife.*[2] This was a serious law. There would be no turning back after the entire kingdom read the edict.

We know how important laws are. We also know how dangerous they can be if not stewarded well. Tomorrow we'll look into God's law and see what effect it produced. But today, let's linger for a moment on what just happened in Esther's world and how the heart behind a law can affect obedience. A law does not have the ability to change our hearts. Only love does that. The ridiculousness of King A.'s edict was not only that it was birthed from an angry, knee-jerk reaction, but it possibly created more havoc in homes rather than harmony. Fear never strengthened a relationship. This brings up a question. Why do you obey God? Is it out of fear or has loved changed you? (Meditate on that question for a while. We will study scripture on it tomorrow.)

JOURNAL

Has an order from a family member or co-worker commanded out of anger and pride made you angry? What did you do? Did you perform the required "duty" happily or with a sulk? Or did you refuse completely? What happened to your heart in the process? Write down your story.

This is the power of journaling. When I write down my hurt, I find I can close the journal, and give it to God. There's just something about writing it down and closing the book. Just as God redeemed this prideful, angry decree by opening the door for a Jewish queen, so I believe He can redeem your situation if He hasn't already. When people of authority command orders out of anger and pride, it's hard to obey without a piece of our hearts dying along the way. Let's pray for God's redemption and restoration of hurting hearts.

HOLD HIS HAND

"Dear Father, you know how a piece of my heart died each time I was forced to obey a rule or order from someone who commanded my obedience out of anger rather than love. I pray you redeem each time this has happened. Turn it for good. Make me more loving and kinder to those under my authority. Don't let ugly pride influence my actions. Amen."

QUESTION FOR GROUP DISCUSSION

Share a time when pride stirred anger in you. How did it turn out?

SOMETHING TO PONDER

Why do you obey God? Is it out of fear or has loved changed you?

A DIFFERENT KIND OF LAW

Yesterday, we briefly discussed the power and importance of a law as we discussed the edict sent out concerning Vashti and the authority of all men in their homes. This is what I wrote:

"A law does not have the ability to change our hearts. Only love does that. The ridiculousness of King A.'s edict was not only that it was birthed from an angry, knee-jerk reaction, but it possibly created more havoc in homes rather than harmony. Fear never strengthened a relationship. This brings up a question. Why do you obey God? Is it out of fear or has loved changed you?"

Let's jump into the scriptures today as we focus on laws, more importantly, God's law. This is essential to understand *whose* we are and how *who we are in Him* affects our purpose in our world. Remember, all scripture is connected. Esther's story reveals the heart of God and the bigger picture of salvation.

⬡ DAILY READING

Read Romans 7:7–14

What did the law do? Did it bring death? What did? (v. 13).

This can be such a confusing scripture, so just in case it's a little fuzzy, I'll try to explain the way I understand it. Paul explained that the purpose of the law was to reveal sin. We wouldn't know good from bad without a law. The law itself doesn't make us bad; it makes us aware.

What separates us from God is the sinful nature in us—selfishness, distrust, and pride. This nature doesn't obey the law because it wants to do its own thing. It wants its way.

God's law was good, but it couldn't change our hearts. Only one thing could do that. And that one thing is love.

Read Ezekiel 36:26–27. What does God promise and what will the Spirit do?

Read Romans 8:1–4. (I love these verses!) Why is there no condemnation (judgment) for those who have trusted Jesus as Savior, and how has God done what the law couldn't do? How has He changed us?

Read Romans 8:14–17. Who are those who allow the Spirit to lead, and what must they do to be glorified in Him? What do you think that suffering looks like?

If I'm honest, the question of how we suffer with Christ has always baffled me. I would love to read your answers and discuss this with you. My initial thoughts of Christ's suffering go to the Cross, to his physical suffering. But along my faith journey, I've found I relate to the emotional suffering of Jesus. People rejected Him. They didn't trust Him or receive what He had to share.

If you've been rejected by those in authority in the church, or you've felt forsaken by God, you've suffered with Christ.

The religious leaders were the ones who refused to acknowledge Him. But Jesus also felt abandoned by God as He hung on the cross. We know the rest of the story. We know the Father did not forsake the Son to the grave, and hopefully, you've experienced that God has not left you either. Yet, if you've been rejected by those in authority in the church, or you've felt forsaken by God, you've suffered with Christ.

Though this verse promises we will share in the sufferings of Christ, it also promises we will be *glorified with* him. These words are translated from the Greek word *sundoxazo* (soon-dox-ad☒'-zo) which interestingly is only used in this verse.

WORD STUDY

GLORIFIED - Greek Strong's Number G4888

συνδοξάζω **syndoxázō,** *soon-dox-ad'-zo; from G4862 and G1392; to exalt to dignity in company (i.e. similarly) with:— glorify together.*

I think this is amazing. The meaning of syndaxo further reveals the heart of our Savior and God. Christ alone should be glorified, but He shares this glory with us.

Read John 17:20–23. Why has Christ given the believers His glory?

"So that we would be one and the world would know that you sent me and loved them as you loved me."

I'm writing this study during a time when our country faces a pandemic, economic downfall, and political and racial division threatening to tear us apart. Now more than ever the Church needs to be unified.

✏ JOURNAL

Read John 17:25–26 three times then turn it into your own prayer.

✋ HOLD HIS HAND

"Holy Father, help me know you more and more each day. Help me become more aware and receptive of your love and grace. I want to be led by your Spirit not my selfish nature. If I suffer, Lord, may it be for your glory. Let any suffering I encounter make you shine through me so the world will know You. Amen."

☕ QUESTION FOR GROUP DISCUSSION

What can we do as the Church to let the world know God's love for them?

REMEMBERED

I know there were many times my kids prayed their mom or dad would forget what happened in the car on the way home. Whether short trips driving back from the mall or travelling across country to see Grandma and Grandpa, inevitably, someone would make his brother or sister angry. They would sit too close, or whine too long, or start an argument quickly escalating until the ruckus would be silenced with a promise. That guarantee would include some form of punishment. To their dismay, we never forgot, and the vow became reality.

One night when we arrived home after a short drive from church, my son Drew was the one in trouble. With great five-year-old wisdom, he asked if he could go to the bathroom first, and his daddy allowed the request. We waited. And waited. And waited for a long time.

Finally, my husband ordered him to come out. When Drew finally opened the door, he was given the punishment promised, but it wasn't as severe as he'd feared. A little time for Dad to cool off was helpful, and the humor of the event couldn't be abated. We pictured him stuffing his pants with toilet paper or something. Years later we learned he was trying to climb out the window, but he couldn't get it open. When that happened, he was hoping if he stayed in there long enough we'd forget about him, but we didn't.

DAILY READING

Esther 2:1–4

Does it seem strange to you that the king forgot what happened? Verse one says he "remembered" Vashti, what she had done and what was decreed. How would you explain this "remembering?"

In the past, I've read this verse and pictured a very hung-over king "remembering" what happened after he came out of his drunken stupor. But remember, we learned last week he was in "good spirits," but not necessarily drunk when he ordered Vashti to come to the party and show her beauty. If he wasn't that drunk, then what does it mean that he "remembered" her? There is an answer to this mystery revealed by Hebrew idioms. These are words or phrases that mean something other than the literal translation. We have idioms in our language too like, "She's under the weather today." We know we're really saying she is sick, right?

WORD STUDY

When "remember" is used in Hebrew it often means that the person "remembering" will be taking action. It's not merely a memory thing but a literal act. Read this explanation from compellingtruth.org:

"When the Bible says God 'remembered,' the original Hebrew verb is zakar (zaw-kar'). Zakar does mean 'to remember,' but it also means 'to bring someone to mind and then act upon that person's behalf.' The Hebrew idea of remembering always includes acting on behalf of the one brought to mind."[3]

So, when the king remembered, it meant he would be taking action on the whole debacle. Which he did. The king's council of young men had a grand plan to replace the queen.

This term is used with God too. Read Jeremiah 31:34. What is the promise?

CHANGE YOUR WORLD

Bless somebody today. If you are in a drive-thru, pay for the person behind you.

According to our new understanding of "remember," does this mean God actually forgets our sins? What does it mean?

Read Luke 1:54–55. When Mary and Elizabeth, both filled with the spirit, prophesied and praised God for the blessing of the Messiah in her womb, Mary cried, "He has helped his servant Israel, in remembrance of his mercy…" What was the action taken, the tangible memory of his mercy?

I think this is so amazing. Acting upon His mercy, God sent His Son to be born under the Bethlehem stars, the perfect Lamb of God, the flawless sacrifice for sin. Did you know that many theologians believe Jesus was born in the special stable used specifically for the sacrificial lambs?

This shepherd's field lay near Bethlehem only five miles from Jerusalem and the Temple. When the angel appeared to the shepherds and promised a baby wrapped in swaddling *cloths* (not *clothes*), lying in a manger, the angel's words were a clue. The shepherds would know where to go because in this field, after the lambs were inspected carefully by the priestly shepherds to verify their perfection, they were wrapped in special *cloths* to prevent injury and insure cleanliness.

Unable to find a room in the inn, Mary and Joseph found themselves exactly where God wanted them to be. It was the cleanest stable in town, and a perfect, sterile swaddling blanket was provided. It's these little details, so symbolic, so powerful, that get me. God does not miss one amazing element to the story.

I know we've not focused on Esther much today, but this is a critical word to understand as we read our Bibles and come to know God better. Read Romans 8:1–2. Rewrite verse 1 replacing "condemnation" with the word "judgment." How does this truth connect with what we've learned today about "remembering?"

JOURNAL

We often think forgiveness means we should forget the offense or hurt someone has inflicted on us because we've interpreted scripture about God's forgiveness this way. But now that you know "remembering" means to act on something, write down how you can forgive someone even though you can't forget their actions. You may want to turn this into a prayer.

HOLD HIS HAND

"Dear Father, Thank You for Your forgiveness. Thank You for "forgetting" our sin because of Your great kindness, mercy, and grace. Please help me live in such a way. Help me remember offenses no more. Help me give them to You. Amen."

☕ QUESTION FOR GROUP DISCUSSION

I wonder if Mary felt forgotten by God when there was no room in the inn. I would've been close to a melt-down. And I wonder if Mary ever looked back at that night in awe of what God had done, all the details. Has there been a time in your life when you felt forgotten by God, but later you were able to see He had a purpose and plan? He did remember you.

DAY 4
PURIFIED

*Later when King Xerxes' fury had subsided, he remembered Vashti and what she had done and what he had decreed about her. Then the king's personal attendants proposed, "Let a search be made for beautiful young virgins for the king. Let the king appoint commissioners in every province of his realm to bring all these beautiful young women into the harem at the citadel of Susa. Let them be placed under the care of Hegai, the king's eunuch, who is in charge of the women; and let **beauty treatments** be given to them. Then let the young woman who pleases the king be queen instead of Vashti." This advice appealed to the king, and he followed it* (Esther 2:1–4 NIV emphasis mine).

Being chosen for this Persian beauty pageant sounds dreamy—except the part about spending the night in the king's bed. But that's another lesson. If you were a beautiful young virgin, you could participate in the greatest beauty pageant of the land. And if you were chosen to compete, then you experienced beauty treatments right away.

I'm all for a day at the spa. I've never had an entire day, but I'm considering putting it on my bucket list. We imagine that these women experienced what we would today, special oils and cosmetics. Maybe mud baths and steam rooms. But I think you're in for a surprise as we study the Hebrew word we've translated as "cosmetics" or "beauty treatments." The ancient word is *tamruwq* (tam-rook ☒). It was a word associated with purification rather than beautifying. The definitions include scraping and rubbing. Maybe rubbing doesn't sound so bad. I love a good massage, but I'm not too sure about the scraping part.

Do the treatments sound wonderful now? How does the meaning of *tamruwq* affect your understanding of what Esther would endure? This isn't a Cinderella story anymore. These beauty treatments take the cliché "Pain is beauty and beauty is pain" to a whole new level.

Before we go further into the story of Esther, I want us to spend some time today focusing on God's kingdom. When we walk into the Kingdom of God, no scraping will be required; however, we are purified to be with our King.

≈ DAILY READING

Read Hebrews 12:28–29. Write down what kind of kingdom are we receiving.

The NIV and ESV translate this verse as "a kingdom that cannot be *shaken*." King James translated it as "a kingdom that cannot be *moved*." I think he wins the translation choice here. Read through the definitions of the Greek word in question:

SHAKEN or MOVED - Greek Strong's Number G761

ἀσάλευτος **asáleutos,** *as-al'-yoo-tos; from G1 (as a negative particle) and a derivative of G4531; unshaken, i.e. (by implication) immovable (figuratively):—which cannot be moved, unmovable.*

The definition uses "unmovable" three times. If "cannot be moved" is the better translation, what does it mean for a kingdom to be moved? If you've studied world history or biblical history, you've read about the rising and falling of power between nations. That's the movement of nations. It is still happening today. I found an interesting article of the moving of nations written only a few months ago. Here's an excerpt:

God has consistently moved through kings and rulers, tribes and nations, disastrous exiles and amazing miracles. Was it a coincidence that just as the huge Jewish population of Spain were being expelled that Columbus sailed the ocean blue, opening the door to a new safe haven? Or that the Romans just happened to have laid fantastic infrastructure throughout their huge empire in time for the Apostles to go on the road with the gospel? Is it unrelated that, despite plans for a Jewish state being long established and waves of Jewish immigrants already arriving, the reestablishment of Israel took place right after the Holocaust? It's hard to say that these remarkable co-incidences were due to God's handiwork with absolute certainty, but the Bible shows how God can and will orchestrate world events to carry out His greater purposes.[4]

No other kingdom can move God's Kingdom. No other king can take King Jesus' place. There is no threat of mutiny or defeat of the Kingdom of God. Yet, God Himself moves kingdoms.

The good news of Jesus is that the Kingdom of God has come into our world. It is here. We are living in the middle of the now and not yet. Jesus hasn't returned to take final control and authority, but the Kingdom of God has entered our space. In a world of constant political strife, wars, and power struggles, isn't it nice to know that with each day passing, the Kingdom of God is here? It lives within us. As we begin to allow His life to take over ours and we share this Good News with our neighbors, His Kingdom gains strength and power in this realm.

Read Hebrews 12:28–29 again. What does the writer of Hebrews tell those receiving the kingdom to do? Why?

"To them God has chosen to make known among the Gentiles the glorious riches of this mystery, which is Christ in you, the hope of glory."

COLOSSIANS 1:27 NIV

Read Hebrews 10:19–23. How do we enter the Most Holy Place?

How are we purified in order to stand before the king? (v. 22)

Whoever wrote the book of Hebrews (some think it could have been Priscilla) wrote specifically to Jewish Christians. That is why the entire book is filled with reference to the Temple and God's history with His people. The portions of scripture in Hebrews 10 and 12 refer to the covenant God made with Moses and the Israelites. The language resembles Exodus 24. Here's a portion of Exodus 24. As you read this Old Testament passage, underline any imagery/language we just read in Hebrews 10 and 12.

> *When Moses went and told the people all the Lord's words and laws, they responded with one voice, "Everything the Lord has said we will do." Moses then wrote down everything the Lord had said. He got up early the next morning and built an altar at the foot of the mountain and set up twelve stone pillars representing the twelve tribes of Israel. Then he sent young Israelite men, and they offered burnt offerings and sacrificed young bulls as fellowship offerings to the Lord. Moses took half of the blood and put it in bowls, and the other half he splashed against the altar. Then he took the Book of the Covenant and*

read it to the people. They responded, "We will do everything the Lord has said; we will obey." Moses then took the blood, sprinkled it on the people and said, "This is the blood of the covenant that the Lord has made with you in accordance with all these words."

…When Moses went up on the mountain, the cloud covered it, and the glory of the Lord settled on Mount Sinai. For six days the cloud covered the mountain, and on the seventh day the Lord called to Moses from within the cloud. To the Israelites the glory of the Lord looked like a consuming fire on top of the mountain. Then Moses entered the cloud as he went on up the mountain. And he stayed on the mountain forty days and forty nights (Exodus 24:3–8, 15–18 NIV).

I find it so exciting and interesting when I realize how much the Old and New Testaments belong together. So many things we do not understand in the New is because we haven't connected it to the Old.

Let's go back to Hebrews. Read Hebrews 10:23. What must we hold onto and why should we hold onto this?

JOURNAL

Write out your confession of hope (confident expectation of good.) This is what you must cling to when hard times come.

HOLD HIS HAND

"Jesus, I praise You, I worship You. You and the Father alone are *faith-*

ful, completely trustworthy. Oh Lord, thank You that You don't rule over us as King A. ruled over his kingdom. His was a kingdom of insecurity, but I am secure in Jesus. Thank You for Your blood that purifies me and makes me whole and holy. Please strengthen my hope. Amen."

☕ QUESTION FOR GROUP DISCUSSION

Discuss the way we worship in our churches today. Do we need to bring reverence and awe back? If so, how do we do that?

NO LONGER FREE

I can only imagine what it's like to be held as a prisoner and unable to visit family and friends—to be limited to only one room or building, to never see the sunrise or sunset or pick up an order of chicken tenders from Chick-fil-A when I please. I know I take my freedom for granted. I'd venture to say most of us do. So, it helps to read the perspective of someone who's endured such loss. Here's a portion of Corrie Ten Boom's story in the concentration camps when she first arrived.

> *"One of my cellmates had spent three years here in Scheveningen. She could hear the rattle of the meal cart long before the rest of us and tell by the footstep who was passing in the corridor. 'That's the trusty from the medical supply. Someone's sick'... 'This is the fourth time someone in 316 has gone for a hearing.'*
>
> *Her world consisted of this cubicle and the corridor outside—and soon I began to see the wisdom of the narrowed vision, and why prisoners instinctively shied away from questions about their larger lives..."[5]*

Corrie goes on to explain that to talk about her life outside the prison would focus her mind on her loved ones and send her thoughts into endless worry and loss. To focus only on what was in front of her was a means of survival, mental stability. The loss of freedom and the worry of loved ones was too great to bear.

I'm not sure if Esther employed this tactic too. Though we glamorize this story, and we know she had favor, digging deeper into the text will help us see this wasn't all fun and games. None of these beautiful girls' lives would ever be the same.

"But those who hope in the LORD will renew their strength. They will soar on wings like eagles; they will run and not grow weary, they will walk and not be faint."

ISAIAH 40:31 NIV

DAILY READING

Read Esther 2:8

> *"So when the king's order and his edict were proclaimed, and when many young women were gathered in Susa the citadel in custody of Hegai, Esther also was taken into the king's palace and put in custody of Hegai, who had charge of the women."*

According to the ESV translation, the women were taken to the "citadel." What is a citadel? Look it up and write the definition.

Who was "in charge" or held "custody" of these contestants? We talked about him a few days ago.

King James calls Hegai the "keeper" of the women. He was their guard. He held constant watch over them night and day. Here's the ancient definition of Hegai's role.

WORD STUDY

KEEPER - Hebrew Strong's Number H8104

שָׁמַר **shâmar,** *shaw-mar'; a primitive root; properly, to hedge about (as with thorns), i.e. guard; generally, to protect, attend to, etc.:—beward, be circumspect, take heed (to self), keep(-er, self), mark, look narrowly, observe, preserve, regard, reserve,* *save (self), sure, (that lay) wait (for), watch(-man).*

I like the idea of protection, but the definition also implies that the women were not allowed to leave. Whether Hegai was protecting or guarding the women to ensure they not escape, my mind pictures him with muscles and strength now rather than a repulsive, shriveled-up old man.

Read Esther 2:12–14. Were they free to go home if the king did not choose them? Where did they go?

I think that is the hardest thing to grasp about this whole story. These young women would never be able to return home even if they weren't chosen. They were destined to become concubines of the king. A concubine was a "second hand" wife. She had no rights as a wife did. If the king did not call her again, she remained in the harem, the part of the household where all the women lived, unable to marry or have a family. She was his property.[6] Sex-trafficking is an ancient practice.

Some commentators do not see this as a bad thing. They theorize this as a move upward in society for these women. Maybe I've seen too many movies, or I live too far removed from this culture, or maybe it's because I'm an American, the land of the free, but I can't believe this was a good thing. In my eyes their life was taken from them forever.

How long were they given the beauty treatments before they saw the king?

Why would it be so long? One theory is that this length of time would reveal if any of the young women were pregnant prior to meeting with the king and therefore protect the king from any unwanted pregnancies/children not his own.

Read Esther 2:10–11. These are telling and powerful verses. Why would Mordecai forbid Esther to reveal that she was a Jew, and what does his daily visitation suggest about the contestants' freedom? Is she in danger?

Esther was in danger because she was a Jew. She also had lost her freedom. But God protected her with wisdom and advice from Mordecai and the favor of Hegai. The Lord was faithful.

JOURNAL

Is this different from how you've read this story before? Journal what you've learned today. Take some time to ponder Esther's situation and listen for God's voice. Write down what you hear.

HOLD HIS HAND

"Dear Father, today's lesson reminds me that being a radiant influence isn't always bubbles and butterflies. My calling may put me in difficult, challenging, and possibly dangerous situations. If it does, help me trust you will be my protection just as you were Esther's. Amen."

QUESTION FOR GROUP DISCUSSION

Have you ever been put in a dangerous place while doing God's work? What happened?

WEEK TWO VIDEO NOTES

Week Three

DAY 1

FAVORED

Corrie Ten Boom's sister, Betsie, was a radiant influence everywhere she went. Throughout their story, Corrie writes of her sister's ability to turn the gloomiest place into a warm, inviting room, even in the concentration camps. Corrie wrote:

> *"…I had seen the home Betsie made in Scheveningen. For unbelievably, against all logic, this cell was charming. My eyes seized only a few details as I inched reluctantly past. The straw pallets were rolled instead of piled in a heap, standing like little pillars along the walls, each with a lady's hat atop it. A headscarf had somehow been hung along the wall. The contents of several food packages were arranged on a small shelf; I could just hear Betsie saying, "The red biscuit tin here in the center!" Even the coats hanging on their hooks were part of the welcome of that room, each sleeve draped over the shoulder of the coat next to it like a row of dancing children."[1]*

It wasn't Betsie's decorating abilities that influenced her cell. It was her spirit. Forgiveness and grace oozed out of this humble woman. Her kindness affected all around her. I have no doubt that her surrendered trust in God, which made her peaceful, and the fruit of the Holy Spirit living in her cultivated the favor she experienced with the other prisoners. Even Corrie was amazed by Betsie's sweet and gentle spirit. Corrie often compared her faith to her sister's and felt lacking.

I share this story because as we study Esther today, I can't help but wonder what it was about Esther that granted her favor. I know she was beautiful on the outside, but I believe kindness, perhaps humility drew Hegai to her. God's hand was definitely working, but Esther did her part. Could being orphaned have given her empathy for the other girls? Did her family's Jewish faith engrain the importance of generosity and love?

Esther's story reminds me of one of my favorite movies, *Miss Congeniality*. Though not trying to be everyone's favorite, the kindness of Gracie Hart does not go unnoticed. She does not win the coveted pageant crown, but she won something even better, the respect and love of the other contestants. Favor and kindness work that way.

DAILY READING

Read Esther 2:8–10. **Who was pleased with Esther, and who was he according to Esther 2:3?**

The Hebrew word describing Hegai is *sariys* (saw-reece). The root meaning of this word means to *castrate*. Although the ancient Hebrews did not practice castration, the cultures around them did. It's interesting that not all *sariys* were eunuchs. This term was used for high officials as well, but more often than not these officials were eunuchs.

According to Matthew Henry, this procedure was often performed early enough in a boy's life to have the most hormonal affect, and he described the men in Hegai's position as "repulsive old men, on whom the court ladies were very dependent, and whose favor they were always desirous to secure."[2] I guess it makes sense that the king would employ an older, "repulsive" man for this role. Yet, the other day as I told a friend I was writing a Bible study on Esther, she said, "Oh, the eunuchs are my favorite. They played a key role in the story."

I'm indebted to her insight. If it hadn't been for her statement, I might have rushed right past dear Hegai never giving a thought to his circumstances. At one point in his life, probably as a young boy, he was chosen to serve the king at a great cost. He would never marry nor enjoy fatherhood, a piece of him was stolen, his original God-given identity taken away, but God used his loss for good.

Read Esther 2:9. What did Hegai do for Esther? How did he use his position as leverage?

We're jumping ahead for a moment, but I think this verse is telling of Esther's character and is a clue to the favor she experienced. Read Esther 2:15. Write down what characteristics most likely caught Hegai's attention and favor.

Define "favor" as best suited for this context (Esther 2:9).

The word "favor" was translated from one of my favorite Hebrew words, *chesed*. We do not have a perfect counterpart. Notice the different nuances of this word.

WORD STUDY

FAVOR - Hebrew Strong's Number H2617

דֶסֶח **cheçed,** *kheh'-sed; from H2616; kindness; by implication (towards God) piety; rarely (by opposition) reproof, or (subjectively) beauty:—favour, good deed(-liness, -ness), kindly, (loving-) kindness, merciful (kindness), mercy, pity,*

Chesed is a Hebrew word that does not have an English counterpart because it means more than love, kindness, or mercy. It's all these things bound by a covenant.

Checed (which is also spelled chesed) is an active, loving kindness bound by a covenant between a wealthier or more capable individual and one who needs help. This further meaning of chesed is demonstrated in many Bible stories such as Ruth's kindness to Naomi and Rahab's kindness to the spies. In Joshua 6, Rahab begs the Israelite spies to return the same "kindness" or *chesed* she had given when she hid them. The spies promised to do so, and when Jericho's walls began crumbling, they saved all of her family. *Chesed* is a Hebrew word that does not have an English counterpart because it means more than love, kindness, or mercy. It's all these things bound by a covenant.

One of the most beloved scriptures that contains *chesed* is Lamentations 3:22. Here are several translations of this familiar promise. I bolded where *chesed* has been translated.

> **NIV-** *"Because of the Lord's great **love** we are not consumed, for his compassions never fail."*

> **ESV-** *"The **steadfast love** of the Lord never ceases; his mercies never come to an end;"*

> **KJV-** *"It is of the Lord's **mercies** that we are not consumed, because his compassions fail not."*

> **NET-** *"The Lord's **loyal kindness** never ceases; his compassions never end."*

Rewrite one of these translations replacing the bolded word(s) with *chesed*. **Now, reread the commentary above explaining this word, and then write your own translation using the definitions of** *chesed*.

JOURNAL

Hegai was exceptionally kind to Esther. He demonstrated mercy and goodness. Have you experienced such *chesed* from a person? Write down your story.

HOLD HIS HAND

"*Chesed* (kheh´-sed) giving God, thank you for your merciful, active kindness and love. Open my eyes to the many times you've given me such favor. Please make me a person more like you and use me to give *chesed* (kheh´-sed) to others. I love you. Amen."

QUESTION FOR GROUP DISCUSSION

Share your answers for question 5 and discuss how changing out the different words in the definition of *chesed* (kheh´-sed) affect the meaning of the scripture.

DAY 2

GOD'S FAVOR

Years ago, when deciding on my college major, I believed God called me into ministry, but that has never looked like I imagined. Rather than shepherding adults in a steepled building, I've found myself shepherding women's hearts through the written word and mentoring middle and high school students teaching literature and writing. Teaching teenagers challenges me to say the least. Some days I love it and feel like I'm making a difference. Other days, I want to quit.

As a teacher, I can share with you who the students are who win my heart. It's not always the brightest or prettiest but the ones who work hard and exude a humble and kind attitude. Those are the kids I would go to the moon for. They're the reason I go to work every day. And though teachers aren't supposed to favor students, those are my favorites.

Yesterday we studied the favor Esther received from Hegai and envisioned what could've granted her such *chesed*. Let's take a moment today to explore other Bible stories of favor. This could give us more clues to Esther's fortune.

DAILY READING

Read Daniel 1:8–16.

What did Daniel do? How was he different from the rest?

Though Daniel and the other young men were given favor with the eunuchs and the king, who ultimately was behind such favor?

Read Luke 2:52. Write this verse in your own words. Does anything about this verse surprise you?

Doesn't it seem Jesus would already have all the favor of the Father? Yet, this verse points to the fact that the favor of God grew even in Jesus' life.

💡 WORD STUDY

Unlike last week's look at "favor," here in Luke 2:52, the Greek word translated as "favor" is the word *charis* (khar -́ece). This word comes from the root word *chairo* (kha ́ee-ro) which means to rejoice.

FAVOR - Greek Strong's Number G5463

χαίρω **chaírō,** *khah'-ee-ro; a primary verb; to be "cheer"ful, i.e. calmly happy or well-off; impersonally, especially as salutation (on meeting or parting), be well:—farewell, be glad, God speed, greeting, hail, joy(- fully), rejoice.*

I love that joy is at the heart of this grace, and it stirs joy in the heart of the recipient.

Can you think of a time when you extended such favor or grace to someone? Why did that person gain your favor?

I haven't read your answer, but I'm guessing the person you favored made you smile. There was something about them that gave you joy. But even if your favor was simply out of the goodness of your heart, giving it probably gave you and the person receiving it joy.

Read 2 Peter 3:18. What does Peter instruct his readers to grow in?

This grace is also *charis* (khar´-ece). Read through the definition above one more time. This will better help us understand Peter's words.

To grow in the grace (*charis*) of God does not mean I need to find more favor with Him. I understand Peter's instruction as encouragement to grow in my thankfulness, joy, and appreciation of what God did for me in Jesus by His loving-kindness.

How different would our lives and our testimony be if we grew in thankfulness and joy to God for our salvation…if every day we were just a little bit more thankful and understood what God did for us on a deeper level? Can we fully wrap our minds around God's mercy? No, but we can grow in that knowledge as we study and cling close to him.

In the same way, by God's loving kindness, He orchestrated Hegai's favor upon Esther. Something about Esther brought joy to Hegai, and she became his favorite. This is a picture of how God loves us. This is grace—God's *chesed*, lovingkindness, mercy, and undeserved favor. It's not earned, it's simply given. We were given this grace in Jesus because God wanted to give it to us. It was His plan from the very beginning. I believe He gave us such grace simply because it brought Him joy.

JOURNAL

Write a prayer of thanksgiving for His favor on you.

Grow in your thankfulness, joy, and appreciation of what God did for you in Jesus because of His loving-kindness.

HOLD HIS HAND

"Dear God, I worship you. I come before you knowing I've not done anything special to receive Your favor, Your *chesed* (kheh´-sed)—You've simply given it to me. It's so sweet to know that I bring You joy. I make You smile. Help me grow in my knowledge of You and in *charis* (khar´-ece), joyful grace, thankfulness for all You've done in Jesus. Amen."

QUESTION FOR GROUP DISCUSSION

How does knowing the meaning of *charis* change your understanding of 2 Peter 3:18? How will this change the way you live today?

DAY 3

SUMMONED BY NAME

One day I walked into a hotel exhausted from an eight-hour solo drive.

"Name?" asked the friendly desk clerk.

Fumbling with my bags I responded, "Lee."

Without missing a beat, he said, "Oh! Andy Lee?"

It always awakens my senses when someone I don't know somehow knows my name—not that it happens very often, but when it does, I'm taken aback. My face must have given away my thoughts, and he explained he'd just spoken with the conference director and read over the list of attendees. Even though the list was fresh on his mind, I liked him. He knew my name.

Our names are important to us. It's nice to be known and painful when we're not. When we feel invisible, forgotten, unwanted. Names played an important role in Esther's story, and they are important in our story with God. My friends, He knows your name.

DAILY READING

Read Esther 2:12–13. The regular period for beautifying was twelve months. This amount of time was divided into different beauty treatments. What were they and for how long?

💡 WORD STUDY

If there were any doubt what these young women were forced to do when they met the king, a study into the ancient language and the connotation behind the words will bring clarity. Her mind and wit would not likely play a large role in this contest—only her body and performance.

In week two we studied the word tamruwq (tam-rook´) from verse 3. Though it's often translated as "beauty treatments," we discovered that the treatments involved scraping rather than simply putting on eyeliner. In the same way, the word beautifying (purifications in the King James) in verse 12 also holds a hidden meaning.

BEAUTIFYING - Hebrew Srong's Number H4838

קוּרמָ mârûwq, *maw-rook'; from H4838; properly, rubbed; but used abstractly, a rubbing (with perfumery):—purification.*

This doesn't sound bad, but the oil had a purpose beyond hydrating dry skin. According to The Jewish Study Bible, the oil rubbed into their skin was myrrh, and this oil was associated with love making.[3] **Read Esther 2:13. What could the young women take to the palace?**

Does this seem odd to you? What would she take? Her pillow? Her favorite blanket or pajamas? Maybe her hairbrush. A bottle of wine? Candles? Chocolate? A movie from Redbox?

Okay, sorry, I got carried away. But really, does this seem odd to you? What do you think the women might have taken with them?

Read Esther 2:14. When would she go to the palace, and where did she return to? What was this group of women called?

Define concubine. What does the definition of concubine tell you about the events of her night with the king?

This contest involved having sex with the king which "married" the contestants to him. Only one woman would become the queen. The others would be secondary wives. They could not return to the king unless they were summoned *by name*.

As I read Esther 2:14, the words "by name" jumped out to me. So, that sent me on a little treasure hunt. Always pursue the words God highlights for you.

⚲ WORD STUDY

NAME - Hebrew Strong's Number H8034

שֵׁם **shêm**, *shame; a primitive word [perhaps rather from H7760 through the idea of definite and conspicuous position; compare H8064]; an appellation, as a mark or memorial of individuality; by implication honor, authority, character:—+ base, (in-) fame(-ous), named(-d), renown, report.*

Does anything stand out to you in the definition? As I read this, what really spoke to me was how a name defines the person. Certainly, in this definition the words "memorial of individuality" sends my mind to the king calling the girl who stood out in his memory. That would be significant. There were a lot of contestants.

But names held even more value than memory in biblical days. An author I highly respect concerning biblical times is Lois Tverberg. She writes in her book, *Walking in the Dust of Rabbi Jesus*, "In the ancient Near East, a person's name was intimately linked to his or her identity or reputation."[4] Names had even more significance than they do now even though today our name and how it's called is significant to our hearts. When someone remembers our name, it means a lot to us. It's been that way since the first sunrise.

Names are important to God, too. Did you know He knows your name? Did you know He's going to give you a new one?

Look up these scriptures and write down the thoughts that come to your mind.

Isaiah 43:1

Revelation 2:17

It's God's character to call us by name. Though the first scripture speaks to Israel, and we must acknowledge that before we apply it to ourselves, that is the kind of God He is, a personable one.

"Fear not, for I have redeemed you; I have summoned you by name; you are mine. When you pass through the waters, I will be with you; and when you pass through the rivers, they will not sweep over you. When you walk through the fire, you will not be burned; the flames will not set you ablaze."

ISAIAH 43:1-2 NIV

JOURNAL

Write down what it would mean to you to hear God summon you by name.

HOLD HIS HAND

"Dear God, it's amazing to think that somehow among all the billions of people on the planet you know me. You not only know me; you know my name. I love that you know it, but I'm even more excited about the day when you will hand me a white stone with a new name only the two of us will share. It will be our secret. You are an intimate, caring, loving God and worthy of my praise. I love you. Amen."

QUESTION FOR GROUP DISCUSSION

Share what spoke to you in this lesson.

DAY 4
GOD'S COMPASSION

There was another king in the Bible who had too many wives. His name was Solomon. Both The Song of Solomon and Esther are included in *The Five Scrolls* which are part of the third major section of The Tanakh, the Hebrew Bible. *The Five Scrolls* are read during Jewish holidays. They include Ruth, Esther, The Song of Solomon, Ecclesiastes, and Lamentations. A rabbi reads from literal scrolls on which each book has been hand-written.

"The Song of Solomon (Song of Songs) is read on the sabbath of Passover week, the Book of Ruth on Shavuot [Pentecost], Lamentations of Jeremiah on Tisha be-Av [Days of Mourning], Ecclesiastes on the sabbath of the week of Sukkoth [The Feast of Tabernacles], and the Book of Esther on Purim."[5]

The Song of Solomon is a love story. Many theologians believe it was written by Solomon himself and is only to be interpreted literally as a love story between a man and a woman. But others believe that this book is allegorical. They maintain it was written by Solomon by the inspiration of the Holy Spirit to paint the picture of God's love for Israel and his love for the Church as the *bride* of Christ.

DAILY READING

Read Song of Solomon 1:1–4. **List words or phrases found in the story of Esther.**

Read Song of Solomon 2:8–17. What name does the bride call the bridegroom? (v. 8–10 and v. 16,17). What names does the bridegroom call the bride? (v.10–15)

What season is it? Is there significance to this season?

Spring is the season of hope and promise. The season of new life. The season we celebrate Jesus' resurrection.

Read Isaiah 54:4–8. What names does God use to describe Himself, and what names or phrases does He use to describe Israel?

What does God promise?

💡 WORD STUDY

"'In a surge of anger I hid my face from you for a moment, but with everlasting kindness I will have compassion on you,' says the LORD your Redeemer" (Isaiah 54:8 NIV, emphasis mine).

Kindness…can you guess what Hebrew word? I bet you can. It's my favorite word, chesed. Here's the definition from Week 2:

> חֶסֶד **cheçed,** *kheh'-sed; from H2616; kindness; by implication (towards God) piety; rarely (by opposition) reproof, or (subjectively) beauty:—favour, good deed(-liness, -ness), kindly, (loving-) kindness, merciful (kindness), mercy, pity…*

Remember, *chesed* is an active loving-kindness bound by a covenant. *Chesed* is often given to those who cannot return the favor. According to this scripture and many others, God's *chesed* is everlasting.

God's merciful loving kindness is everlasting. His chesed never ends.

Everlasting. Stop for a moment and take a deep breath in. Let it out slowly and then read this sentence out loud: "God's merciful loving kindness is everlasting. His *chesed* never ends."

God also promises His *compassion*.

Compassion was translated from *râcham* (raw-kham'.) Our English word does not fully reveal its meaning either.

Circle what God highlights for you in this definition:

COMPASSION - Hebrew Strong's Number H7356

> סחַם **racham,** *rakh'-am; from H7355; compassion (in the plural); by extension, the womb (as cherishing the fetus); by implication, a maiden:—bowels, compassion, damsel, tender love, (great, tender) mercy, pity, womb.*

Years ago I found this word in one of my quiet times. I remember the word "womb" jumping into my spirit. Is there a safer or more loving place than a mother's womb? I love this description of God's compassion for us.

Hebrew language is visual. Each letter in the alphabet forms a picture that gives it meaning. So it is with the meaning of Hebrew words, and *racham* is a good example of this. I do not think you can separate the image of the womb from *racham*. When it is spoken or written, it evokes the image of a place of safety, protection, and growth. That place is smack-dab in the center of God's merciful compassion.

JOURNAL

Do you struggle with assurance of God's racham for you, His tender, sympathetic, and loving compassion? If so, did you have a parent whom you could never please or often got angry and held grudges? This could be why it's hard to believe and receive God's love. God is not like your earthly parent. Write a prayer asking for His supernatural grace to release your heart from past wounds so you can accept His compassion for you today. You'll never be the same.

HOLD HIS HAND

"Dear heavenly Father, I praise you! You are such a wonderful, loving Father. I pray I may grow in understanding of this piece of your nature. Help me never doubt your racham (raw-kham') again, because I cannot give to others what I have not accepted for myself. Amen."

QUESTION FOR GROUP DISCUSSION

Did the Word Study today enrich your understanding of the scripture in Isaiah or confuse you? Discuss your different experiences. No judgment zone!

DAY 5
THE BRIDE OF CHRIST

We've been going back and forth from Esther to other scripture, and today we should be returning to Esther, but we have one more piece to cover before we can go back to her story. *Radiant Influence* is a study of Esther, but my heart behind this study and every book I write is for you to dive deeper into the love of God. Your radiant influence will flow from a heart soaked in the truth of His love for you. So, let's continue a little further before we go back to Esther.

We left her in Day 3 where we uncovered what would happen to each girl after she slept with the king. He would be a man with many "extra" wives. This led me to Solomon and to the Song of Songs which led to God's love. The Isaiah scripture held imagery of God loving Israel as a Husband as well as merciful, compassionate parent. Today, we're coming back to the imagery of marriage and the Church as the Bride of Christ. This too is paramount in our identity and from where our influence will flow.

DAILY READING

Read 2 Corinthians 11:2. What does Paul state he did for the Corinthians?

Read Ephesians 5:25–27. How did Christ "love" the church? Why did he do this?

Go back to Song of Solomon which we studied yesterday and read 4:7. Describe the bride.

Read Revelation 19:6–9. Why are they rejoicing?

"Let us rejoice and exult and give him the glory, for the marriage of the Lamb has come, and his Bride has made herself ready; it was granted her to clothe herself with fine linen, bright and pure"— for the fine linen is the righteous deeds of the saints (Revelation 19:7–8).

At first glimpse, "the righteous deeds" conveys that those saints were "good enough." The church had "made herself ready." But that is contradictory to what we've been studying. We know we can't do enough good things to get into heaven. We only enter through the blood of Christ. So, let's do a little digging.

ⓦ WORD STUDY

RIGHTEOUS DEEDS - Greek Strong's Number G1345

δικαίωμα **dikaíōma**, *dik-ah'-yo-mah; from G1344; an equitable deed; by implication, a statute or decision:—judgment, justification, ordinance, righteousness.*

Circle the words decision, judgment, justification, and ordinance.

Now read how King James translates this verse:

"And to her was granted that she should be arrayed in fine linen, clean and white: for the fine linen is the righteousness of saints" (Revelation 19:8 KJV, emphasis mine).

Do you see the difference? King James simply translated dikaíōma as the righteousness of the saints where the ESV reads as the righteous deeds of the saints. I feel it is very important to understand the difference here. While you can see why ESV would use the word deeds because the word appears in the definition, we must align with the entire narrative of God's Word. Our righteous deeds don't get us into heaven; it is only by the decision, justification, and ordinance of God that He declared in Jesus.

Hold that thought as we study the word *saints*.

SAINTS - Hebrew Strong's Number G40

ἅγιος hágios, *hag'-ee-os; from ἅγος hágos (an awful thing) (compare G53, G2282); sacred (physically, pure, morally blameless or religious, ceremonially, consecrated):—(most) holy (one, thing), saint.*

If I retranslated Revelation 19:8 with the definitions of dikaíōma and hágios in mind, I would write:

"the fine linen is the legal right of those who've been made holy and pure through Christ."

How does this change the meaning of Revelation 19:8b from most translations?

What does the angel command John to write in Revelation 19:9?

"Then the angel said to me, 'Write this: Blessed are those who are invited to the wedding supper of the Lamb!' And he added, 'These are the true words of God.'"

REVELATION 19:9 NIV

We are invited. We are not only invited; we are the bride.

Weddings seem to be turning up everywhere I look these days. Yet one day the most beautiful wedding will commence. Jesus is the bridegroom preparing for His bride. We are the Church, the bride preparing for His coming.

Esther spent a year preparing for her "marriage" to the king with the hope that she would be the chosen one.

JOURNAL

Journal your thoughts on the truth that our righteous deeds are not what get us into heaven.

HOLD HIS HAND

"Dear God, thank you for loving me…or desiring me. It's hard to fathom. I can understand why you love others, but sometimes I struggle to believe that you love me. I'm trying to be good enough when you've already done what was needed for my entry into heaven. I am part of the bride of Christ, and one day I will meet you face to face as hagios (hag '-ee-os), a saint, whose beautiful dress was paid for by you—no alterations needed. One size fits all in the kingdom of God. One bride, no secondary ones. I am yours. Let it be so."

QUESTION FOR GROUP DISCUSSION

The imagery of the Church as the bride of Christ is interesting. We often individualize our faith, but we aren't individual brides to Christ, we are a collective bride. How can we help the Church, our fellow sisters and brothers, ready themselves for the bridegroom?

WEEK THREE VIDEO NOTES

Week Four

DAY 1
ACCEPTED AND LOVED

As a military family we moved many times. Each time we relocated I would worry about my kids. It's not easy being the new kids in school. I always prayed a kind child would be inclusive and invite them into his circle of buddies.

It got harder when Mike retired, and we became civilians living in the "outside" world. When you're in the military, everyone is a transplant far from home, but in the world outside of this community, people have roots, childhood friends, and family close by. That makes it harder to be accepted into a group.

My kids were fine. They always seemed to find friends quickly. But I must admit, sometimes it was hard for me. Yes, the momma needed and wanted to fit in too. I especially felt this sitting in the football stands watching my son play lacrosse. Stadiums can be lonely places when they're filled with people.

But one day, a very kind woman invited me to sit with her. Sara had been a lacrosse mom for many years and was close to all the other moms whose sons had played together since junior high. Because of her, I was accepted into the mom group. The stadium was no longer a lonely place.

My kids are grown now, and I never see those lacrosse moms anymore except for Sara. After a decade of living in one place (a record for us), fitting in and being accepted by others isn't something I need. But more importantly, my friendship with Sara has lasted, and we walk together every day. I will always be thankful for her kind heart and eyes able to see someone who needed a friend—even at age forty-two.

I don't know if Esther felt the need to be accepted by the other contestants and the palace workers. I'm not sure if she wanted to be accepted by King A. But I do know that King A. not only accepted her and chose her, some translations say he loved her. And that changes things.

🪶 DAILY READING

Esther 2:15–18. **According the latter part of verse 15, with whom was Esther winning "favor" now?**

💡 WORD STUDY

"Now Esther was winning favor in the eyes of all who saw her" *(Esther 2:15).*

The Hebrew word translated as favor is not the Hebrew word chesed (kheh-sed). The word is chên (khane.)

FAVOR - Hebrew Strong's Number H2580

חֵן **chên** *khane; from H2603; graciousness, i.e. subjective (kindness, favor) or objective (beauty):—favour, grace(-ious), pleasant, precious, (well-) favoured.*

חֶסֶד **cheçed**, *kheh'-sed; from H2616; kindness; by implication (towards God) piety; rarely (by opposition) reproof, or (subjectively) beauty:—favour, good deed(-liness, -ness), kindly, (loving-) kindness, merciful (kindness), mercy, pity.*

Keep in mind that chesed involves a covenant.

How do chên and chesed differ?

I know some might think I'm guilty of splitting hairs when it comes to words, but I feel each word is written with a specific purpose in mind. In my understanding, chên does not involve the relational kindness and mercy that chesed portrays. Chên is what I experienced with the group of lacrosse moms. They accepted me, but my relationship with Sara was rooted in chesed, merciful kindness.

Chên is often superficial. It doesn't always last, but chesed does.

Read Esther 2:16–17. How did the king feel about Esther? Read several translations if you can.

What did Esther "win" from the king and what did he place on her head?

"and she won grace [chên] and favor [chesed] in his sight…" (ESV)

"she won his favor [chên] and approval [chesed]…" (NIV)

Look back at the definitions for chên and chesed and write down their meaning in your own words. Why is it important that she won both from the king?

The king's chên or his acceptance and approval positioned Esther for the future salvation of her people, but his chesed (merciful acts of loving kindness rooted in covenant) prepared his heart to receive Esther later when she wasn't invited.

The king's chên or his acceptance and approval positioned Esther for the future salvation of her people, but his chesed (merciful acts of loving kindness rooted in covenant) prepared his heart to receive Esther later when she wasn't invited. Perhaps Vashti had only received chên from King A., but that was as far as their relationship went. There was no mercy, no acts of loving kindness to change his mind.

EXTRA!

Really quick, I want to point out something I've missed for years. We always read Esther's story quickly, so when we read that the beauty treatments were a year long, we assume a year's time spans between Vashti's and Esther. But that's not the case when you look closely.

Read Esther 1: 1–3. What year is it in King Ahasuerus's reign?

Read Esther 2:16. What year did Esther go to the king?

Wow! Four whole years passed between Vashti's banishment and Esther's night with the king. Who knew?

JOURNAL

Esther probably did not wait four years in the citadel before she saw the king, but the timeline we've uncovered indicates this was a slow process. It didn't happen overnight. We do know she had to wait at least a year, and there is no indication she knew when her name would be called. Are you waiting for anything right now? Write it down and ask the Lord to help you trust His timing.

✋ HOLD HIS HAND

"God of chesed (khes-ed), please help me trust you when I'm lonely and there is no change in sight. While I'm waiting, help me have eyes to see those who need a friend and grant me favor with those around me. Amen."

☕ QUESTION FOR GROUP DISCUSSION

Was it a surprise to realize there were four years between Vashti to Esther? Why could it have taken so long?

CHOSEN

The life of a writer is often plagued with rejection. We send our proposals to acquisition editors, and after waiting for many months, we receive an email either accepting the proposal or rejecting it. Most writers will tell you they've received more rejections than acceptance.

Rejection makes me want to quit or at least climb into my bed and take a long nap under the covers. I usually do recover (when I finally climb out of the covers,) but honestly, it's only by God's grace that I keep on trying.

But God is not like this, my friends. He's not a big acquisition editor or publicity board in the sky weighing whether or not we're a good investment. Just as the king chose Esther, we've been chosen by the King of Kings.

Honestly, we're the ones who reject God. His hand is always extended first. Let me show you scripture to prove it, but first, let's start with Esther.

DAILY READING

According to Esther 2:18, what did the king do after he crowned Esther?

Would this king miss an opportunity to throw a big party? Whose feast was it?

How did the kingdom benefit from the king's choice of a new queen?

WORD STUDY

A history lesson rather than Strong's definitions will enlighten this passage. Read these commentaries:

HOLIDAY, or in some translations, RELEASE

"According to Herodotus, it was customary for the Persian kings, upon their accession to the throne, to remit the tribute which was due to them from all their cities; and Ahasuerus, on this occasion, out of his abundant joy, remitted some tax, or part of a tax, then due, which he did that everybody might rejoice with him."[1]

GIFTS

"The Heb. word was used in older times for a portion of food sent from the table (Genesis 43:34; 2 Samuel 11:8)"[2]

Sometimes I like King A. and other times I don't. I visualize him as a drunken, self-absorbed, heartless man but then I catch a glimpse of his tender side, and I'm reminded of his generosity. Kingships are difficult for us to grasp in this modern democratic society. We rebel against the thought of one man holding so much power.

However, we do understand what it's like to be chosen or not. Many of us know all too well the pain of rejection. We were the last ones to be picked for the team, or we were never asked to play on the team. The king chose Esther out of all the beautiful women to become the new queen, and, my friends, if you are sitting here with me studying the Bible, you and I are chosen women too.

Read John 15:16. Did the disciples choose Jesus or did Jesus choose the disciples?

Ray Vander Laan teaches that in biblical days those desiring to be a disciple watched the rabbis, listened to their teaching, then asked the rabbi of their choice if they could "follow" him. The disciple chose the rabbi. Of course, the rabbi owned the final decision to accept or deny the disciple. But Jesus did this differently. Rather than waiting for disciples to ask, He invited them. He chose them first.

Does this stir anything in your spirit? How would you feel if Jesus came to you and chose you out of the crowd to be a disciple?

Look up the definition of "disciple." Are you a disciple of Jesus? How do you know according to the definition?

If the definition of disciple is a "learner or pupil", and you are in a Bible study learning, I conclude that you are a disciple of Rabbi Jesus.

Read Ephesians 1:3–6. As you read these verses, keep in mind the big picture. Think people groups, Jews and gentiles. Don't get caught up in individual predestination. That's not what this verse means.

Keeping all this in mind, what does it mean to you that God chose us in Him before the foundations of the world? What is significant about this truth?

✏ JOURNAL

Do you feel you chose Jesus or He chose you? Which do you feel came first? Write about it.

✋ HOLD HIS HAND

"Dear Lord, I know rejection. It's an awful feeling. The fact that you invited the disciples first makes me smile. Thank you for inviting, calling me to follow you. Amen."

☕ QUESTION FOR GROUP DISCUSSION

Read Ephesians 1:3–6 together and discuss your answers from question five.

DAY 3

DELAYED REWARDS

When we recall Esther's story, we always think of her position and placement with God's hand in mind. We can see how He orchestrated such events. But Esther isn't the only one who found herself in the right place at the right time to make a difference. Mordecai was there too. Scripture tells us that Mordecai stopped by every day to check on Esther and inquire how she was doing, but there's a chance he wasn't merely taking a stroll through town. Some theologians believe there is evidence that he served as an official at the king's gate.

The name "Mordecai" resembles another Persian name, "Marduka." This name was listed on a cuneiform text that dates back to the early years of King Ahasuerus.[3] This text held the names of the king's officials and scribes. Though no tangible evidence proves that Marduka and Mordecai are one and the same, Mordecai's position "sitting at the king's gate" in Esther 2:21 and again in Esther 3:3, and the level of authority given to him later in the story, certainly provide the possibility. Take a look at those two scriptures before you go to the questions.

We know Mordecai influenced Esther's actions later on, but something else happened involving wise Mordecai that would affect the story down the road. He was in the right place at the right time, but his actions wouldn't seem to make a difference.

⟋ DAILY READING

Read Esther 2:21–22. **Who planned to assassinate the king? Why?**

According to verse 22, how did the king learn of this plot against his life, and in what name did Esther reveal this to the king?

Do you remember what we discussed in week 3, day 3 about using names in biblical times? Why would Esther use Mordecai's name? What does this tell you about Mordecai?

The rest of the story was not good for the men who planned the coup. They were hung on the gallows or impaled on a stake. Statues and drawings from these ancient civilizations as well as historian records prove that the Persians impaled their victims to execute them and then hung them, which served as an exhibition and warning.[4] It was a very cruel time.

Mordecai foiled the plot to assassinate the king, yet the king didn't even say thank you. It was out of character for a Persian king not to immediately and generously reward an act of loyalty. However, even though Mordecai's faithfulness wasn't rewarded, it was recorded.

Read Esther 2:23. Who was in the room when it was recorded?

The king was present. This is important because his presence will stir his memory later. The plot of the story is building, and as in all good stories, the foreshadowing detail of Mordecai's loyalty recorded in the king's records promises the future reward for him. While we're on this subject, let's take a minute to remember what Jesus promised about rewards.

Read Matthew 6:1–6. What does Jesus promise about rewards?

Would you rather have the world's accolades or God's? Do you think His are worth waiting for?

EXTRA!

If you have extra time today, you might enjoy reading these scriptures that also promise God's rewards. Write down your thoughts on each scripture.

2 Corinthians 5:6–10

Revelation 3:1–6

Though we've read about being judged for what we've done, that judgment is not what decides our eternal destiny but rather our rewards in eternity. The Revelation scripture, however, does allude to saints who have not "soiled their garments" whose names will never be blotted out of the book of life and will be confessed by Jesus to the Father. Our relationship with Jesus holds the key to our salvation, but out of that relationship good works will flow. Read this commentary on Revelation 3:1–3 from David Stern:

> *"Today this statement about hypocrites describes people (Jews, Christians, other) who support charitable works but have no spiritual connection with the living God (Isaiah 64:5(6)); people who feel close to God or have correct theo-*

logical doctrine but produce no evangelistic or social action fruit (Ya 2:17); people whose lack of faith in God and ignorance or rejection of Yeshua produce dead religious formalism, social clubbiness, fortress mentality defensiveness, and/ or pride in self-accomplishment; and people try to fill their spiritual vacuum with sensual gratification."[5]

Does anybody want to say, "Ouch!"? Did any of that sting? Are our churches guilty of any of these things? Please remember, our salvation and our works flow out of our relationship with Jesus. Talk to Him. Walk with Him. Study His Word to know Him. Simply, love your Jesus. Mordecai didn't know Jesus, but he had great faith in God. I believe his trust in God gave him peace when the reward from the king did not come.

> "Trust in the Lord with all your heart and lean not on your own understanding; in all your ways submit to him, and he will make your paths straight."
>
> PROVERBS 3: 5-6

✎ JOURNAL

Have you experienced a time when you did not receive the reward you felt you deserved? Are you still waiting? Does it help to trust God as the orchestrater of your position and the rewarder of your faithfulness?

✋ HOLD HIS HAND

"Jesus, King of Kings, help me trust You. You promised that the Father loved the world so much He gave You so that whoever trusts You will not die but live forever. Honestly, Lord, living forever with You is all the reward I want, but I look forward to the day when I kneel at Your feet and hear You call my name written in the book of Life. What a day that will be. Amen."

☕ QUESTION FOR GROUP DISCUSSION

Read the extra scriptures about reward and share what they stir in you.

PERSECUTED FOR FAITH

"After these things King Ahasuerus promoted Haman the Agagite, the son of Hammedatha, and advanced him and set his throne above all the officials who were with him. And all the king's servants who were at the king's gate bowed down and paid homage to Haman, for the king had so commanded concerning him. But Mordecai did not bow down or pay homage. Then the king's servants who were at the king's gate said to Mordecai, "Why do you transgress the king's command?" And when they spoke to him day after day and he would not listen to them, they told Haman, in order to see whether Mordecai's words would stand, for he had told them that he was a Jew. And when Haman saw that Mordecai did not bow down or pay homage to him, Haman was filled with fury. But he disdained to lay hands on Mordecai alone. So, as they had made known to him the people of Mordecai, Haman sought to destroy all the Jews, the people of Mordecai, throughout the whole kingdom of Ahasuerus" (Esther 3:1–6).

Where do I start? This is wrong on so many levels. Are you feeling it? It's amazing how quickly life can disintegrate, how one spark can start an inferno. Mordecai was just doing what Mordecai always did. As a faithful servant of the king and God, he reported the coup and saved the king. Yet, Mordecai didn't receive reward. Ironically, another man received a promotion. Haman rose to power.

Perhaps life would've gone on as normal if the king didn't demand everyone bow to Haman. I'm sure he was trying to help his buddy gain respect, but this was a terrible way to achieve authority. However, all the officials at the king's gate bowed except one.

Mordecai was a man of integrity. He would not bow. Perhaps as the king demanded worship of Haman, a scripture Mordecai recited every day as a small boy played in his mind. The Shema is still prayed every morning and evening by Jewish families. It starts with these words:

> "Hear, O Israel: The LORD our God, the LORD is one. Love the LORD your God with all your heart and with all your soul and with all your strength" (Deuteronomy 6:4–5 NIV).

Mordecai would also have known by heart the first commandment:

> "I am the LORD your God, who brought you out of Egypt, out of the land of slavery. You shall have no other gods before me" (Exodus 20:2–3 NIV).

So, when the king and the arrogant Haman demanded others bow down to him, Mordecai refused. And what started as anger against one man quickly became motive for vengeance on a whole people. Hate and racism are nothing new. They don't make sense now, and they didn't then either.

"Therefore, my dear brothers and sisters, stand firm. Let nothing move you. Always give yourselves fully to the work of the Lord, because you know that your labor in the Lord is not in vain."

1 CORINTHIANS 15:58 NIV

DAILY READING

Read Esther 3:7. What year of the king's reign was it now? How many years was Esther queen before Haman planned revenge upon Mordecai and the Jews?

When we read the story of Esther, and when we watch the Veggie Tale version, it seems as if every event happened the next day. But years had passed.

Do you think the length of time Esther had been queen played a role in the rest of the story? How?

According to Esther 3:7 (NIV), why were the Pur cast?

So…what were the pur? This is what I found in Shepherds Notes:

"The month of Nisan was the first month of the new year, and the custom in Persia called for the casting of lots at that time. Lots were cast to determine which month during the year would be most favorable for significant events."[6]

Crazy isn't it? Or at least it seems bizarre to us, but this was an excepted part of the culture. The Persians "rolled the dice" to make their decision, but other nations and cultures did also, including God's people.

Read Exodus 28:29,30. What did Aaron wear in the "breastpiece of judgment?"

The "Urim and Thummim" are a great mystery. Mentioned only a few times in the Bible, these two objects were used to receive God's guidance. Many believe they were two stones that simply gave "yes" or "no" answers. Some believe they were black and white. When both stone die rolled black, God's answer was no, and when they both rolled white, his answer was yes. The Jewish Virtual Library gives a detailed explanation that includes the twelve stones representing the tribes of Israel:

"Interpreting Urim to mean 'those whose words give light' and

Thummim as 'those whose words are fulfilled,' the rabbis explain that the oracle was effected by rays of light shining on the letters, or protruding from them and forming themselves into groups (Yoma 73b), so that the high priest could read them. Only priests speaking by means of the holy spirit and upon whom the Shekhinah rested could invoke them."[7]

I hope this hasn't confused you too much. Like I said, the Urim and Thummim and the whole breastpiece are great mysteries. Definitely something to dig into for fun (depending on your definition of fun.) But let's get back to Esther.

Read Esther 3:8–11. What does Haman tell the king? How does he describe the people he wants to exterminate, and what does Haman want to be decreed about these people? (v. 9)

💡 WORD STUDY

DESTROYED - Hebrew Strong's Number H6

דבַאָ *'âbad*, *aw-bad'; a primitive root; properly, to wander away, i.e. lose oneself; by implication to perish (causative, destroy):—break, destroy(-uction), not escape, fail, lose, (cause to, make) perish, spend, × and surely, take, be undone, × utterly, be void of, have no way to flee.*

Abad indicates that the Jews would have no way to flee. No escape. This is frightening. They would not be able to run. They were trapped.

How much money does Haman promise the king in return for this destruction, and what is the significance of the king giving Haman his signet ring?

This either shows the king's great trust and faith in Haman or his lackadaisical, apathetic rule. Maybe it shows both. He asks very few questions about the people Haman wants annihilated. In great trust of this man whom he's made powerful, the king gives the stamp of approval, his very own signet ring.

✒ JOURNAL

Read John 19:10–12. Pilate did not want Jesus crucified, yet the Jewish political leaders demanded it. So, Pilate washed his hands, hoping to separate himself from the death of God's Son. Perhaps King A. was washing his hands when he gave his signet ring to Haman rather than using it himself. Write down what comes to mind as you compare these stories.

✋ HOLD HIS HAND

"Father, life can be so unfair, but nothing I go through wasn't also experienced by your people and most of all, Your Son. Evil seems to be so strong. It wants to destroy Your goodness, but You've already written the end of my story. I will not be 'âbad (aw-vad). I will be clothed in immortality. Thank You, Jesus. Thank You, Father. Amen."

☕ QUESTIONS FOR GROUP DISCUSSION

God is not mentioned once in the story of Esther, and He seems to be absent in the scene before Pilate. Where were the angel armies? Why would God let things go this far? It appears that evil is in control. An edict was given to destroy the Jews, and Pilate allowed for Jesus to be destroyed. But death does not win.

Read 1 Corinthians 15:50–57. What is the victory? When will the saying, "O death, where is your sting?" come to pass?

I have read this verse and quoted it many times. When my sister died, I felt the sting of death even though I knew that we will one day be reunited. So, this verse haunted me because I still felt the sting. But studying it again I realized that we will experience the sting of death until we have put on our "immortal skin."

Read 1 Corinthians 15:58. Combine what we've studied in today's lesson of unfairness and persecution. How is this encouraging?

DAY 5
REPENTANCE

Repentance literally means to change the way we think. Change starts with what we believe. Here's the Strong's entry:

3340 metanoéō (from 3326 /metá, "changed after being with" and 3539 /noiéō, "think") – properly, "think differently after," "after a change of mind"; to repent (literally, "think differently afterwards").

What do you need to change in your thinking?

As I write this Bible study in the year 2020, unbelievable things are happening in our country. We're living through a pandemic that has taken many lives and injured our economy. Bizarre weather has occurred from the West coast to the East. Earthquakes have shaken ground that's never experienced tremors. "Fire tornadoes" are a new phenomenon, and something called a "derecho," which is like a hurricane in the middle of the country, caused devastation in the heartland.

If a pandemic and this strange weather were not enough, America faces lawlessness and social unrest with the call to defund the police. It's pretty insane. And frightening. I wonder what people will think when they read these words decades later. I hesitated to begin this lesson this way; an author needs to keep her writing evergreen and pertinent to the next generations, but today's lesson is on repentance, and that's been a big topic among the spiritual leaders as we watch our country being torn apart naturally, spiritually, and politically.

We live on the other side of the Cross where grace abounds. Beyond the need to come to God with a repenting heart when we first surrender to Jesus, we don't focus on this action. I've shied away from it myself. Grace is much easier to preach, but there would be no need for grace if there weren't a holy God who demands justice and holiness. They go together like the double stuff sugary filling and the chocolate cookie of the Oreo. I must be hungry. I better close this introduction, but I'm hoping today's topic will stir some heart searching and good discussion with your group. The bottom line is that God loves us, yet we could learn from Mordecai and the Jewish people how to respond when the battle wages for our lives.

🪶 DAILY READING

Read Esther 4:1–3. **How did Mordecai and the people react when he received the news of the decree? What do you picture when you see the words "sackcloth and ashes?"**

I picture an old farm feed sack, all scratchy and light brown in color, and ashes on their heads. But my visual is not entirely correct—at least the color of the sack. This is very interesting to me:

> "Sackcloth is a coarse, black cloth made from goat's hair that was worn together with the burnt ashes of wood as a sign of mourning for personal and national disaster, as a sign of repentance and at times of prayer for deliverance."[8]

The ashes were sprinkled on their heads. We learn this from the actions of Job's friends when they saw him:

> "When Job's three friends, Eliphaz the Temanite, Bildad the Shuhite and Zophar the Naamathite, heard about all the troubles that had come upon him, they set out from their homes and met together by agreement to go and sympathize with him and comfort him. When they saw him from a distance, they could hardly recognize him; they began to weep aloud, and they tore their robes and sprinkled dust on their heads. Then they sat on the ground with him for seven days and seven nights. No one said a word to him, because they saw how great his suffering was" (Job 2:11–13 NIV).

If only his friends had stayed silent instead of trying to figure out the reason for his suffering. We could learn much from this, but that's another Bible study. Let's keep going.

According to the commentary above, what were sackcloth and ashes a sign of?

Humbling. Can you imagine putting on sackcloth and ashes?

Where did Mordecai sit in his sackcloth and ashes? (v.2) Why could he not go in?

> "…and he went out into the midst of the city, and he cried out with a loud and bitter cry" (Esther 4:1 ESV, emphasis mine).

Do you think he was wailing or speaking?

WORD STUDY

CRIED - Hebrew Strong's Number H2199

זָעַק zâ'aq, zaw-ak'; a primitive root; to shriek (from anguish or danger); by analogy, (as a herald) to announce or convene publicly:—assemble, call (together), (make a) cry (out), come with such a company, gather (together), cause to be proclaimed.

I don't know if he was crying out to God for help or to the other people to repent, or both. There was another man, an exile in a Persian court who also dressed in sackcloth and ashes crying out to God. The book of Daniel gives us deeper insight to this cry.

Read Daniel 9:3–19 Who was Daniel crying out to? Summarize his cry. Why does Daniel have faith that his plea will be heard and acted upon by God? (v. 18)

It's hard for us to comprehend how much the Jewish people believed in their chosen-ness by God. Yet, it was this special relationship that gave them the strength and hope when all seemed hopeless. Their faith ran generational blood-lines deep. They had witnessed His salvation of their ancestors and believed in the merciful and powerful character traits of YHWH. They also knew at times they deserved His anger, but they never doubted they were God's people like so many of us do when trouble comes our way. They didn't question His mercy or His goodness. Rather, they repented of their sins and trusted God's forgiveness.

✎ JOURNAL

I'm feeling the need to repent of our tendency to be mad at God when things go wrong. It's human to be angry with God. Job was. But when God spoke to Job, he too repented. Listen to his change of heart:

Then Job replied to the Lord:

> *"I know that you can do all things, no purpose of yours can be thwarted. You asked, 'Who is this that obscures my plans without knowledge?' Surely I spoke of things I did not understand, things too wonderful for me to know. You said, 'Listen now, and I will speak. I will question you, and you shall answer me.' My ears had heard of you, but now my eyes have seen you. Therefore I despise myself and repent in dust and ashes." - Job 42:1–6 NIV*

Write down your thoughts on repentance. Do you struggle with this, or have you experienced the benefit of repenting and crying out to God?

✋ HOLD HIS HAND

"Father, I'm thankful that you are a forgiving, good God. I live on the other side of the Cross where your goodness and faithfulness culminated. If I ever doubt your goodness again, please forgive me. I repent of my own pride and distrust. Amen."

☕ QUESTION FOR GROUP DISCUSSION

What are your thoughts about repentance? Is it still needed today? What could our equivalent to "sack cloth and ashes" be?

WEEK FOUR VIDEO NOTES

Week Five

DAY 1

FASTING AND TRUSTING

I want to apologize ahead of time. This lesson is a little long, but it's all so very important. I'm skipping the intro today because there's a lot of commentary. Let's jump in. I'm praying for you.

DAILY READING

Read Esther 4:8–9. Summarize what just happened.

Read Esther 4:10–11. **What were Esther's reasons for not obeying Mordecai? How long had it been since she had seen the king? Do you remember how long they had been married?**

They had been married for five years, and she had not seen him for a month. Was the honeymoon over?

Read Esther 4:12–14. Did Mordecai let her off the hook? What were the reasons he gave for her to go to the king despite the danger?

This is probably one of the most famous passages in the Bible—for sure the Old Testament. Mordecai tells her that she will die if she doesn't try to do anything to save her people. So, she's doomed even if she plays it safe and does not go before the king. He also tells her that her family will die, but God will raise up someone to save his people.

And then...he says these renowned words. Consider these translations:

> ESV- *"And who knows whether you have not come to the king-*dom *for such a time as this?" (emphasis mine.)*

> NIV- *"...to your* royal position *for such a time as this?" (emphasis mine.)*

Let's do some digging. Discrepancies in translations always get me excited.

💡 WORD STUDY

ROYAL POSITION - Hebrew Strong's Number H4438

מַלְכוּת malkûwth, *mal-kooth'; or* תְּבְלַמ *malkuth; or (in plural)* הָיֻכְלַמ *malkuyâh; from H4427; a rule; concretely, a dominion:—empire, kingdom, realm, reign, royal.*

The root of the word royal is Malak. - Hebrew Strong's Number H4427

וּךְלָמ mâlak, *maw-lak'; a primitive root; to reign; inceptively, to ascend the throne; causatively, to induct into royalty; hence (by implication) to take counsel:—consult, × indeed, be (make, set a, set up) king, be (make) queen, (begin to, make to) reign(-ing), rule, × surely.*

Can you imagine being an ordinary girl one minute and a queen the next? Usually, queens and kings rise to such power through their family line. They know it's coming. They're groomed to step into such a position, but this was not Esther's story.

Do you think Esther viewed herself as royal or ordinary? Do you think she realized the power she had at that time? Why? Please tuck those thoughts in the back of your mind for tomorrow.

Once Esther made up her mind to step into her role as the queen, everything changed. It seems one minute, she was full of fear; the next, she was rising to the occasion and assuming her authority—even over the man who raised her. She gave Mordecai instructions. I love her spunk.

> Then Esther told them to reply to Mordecai, "Go, gather all the Jews to be found in Susa, and hold a fast on my behalf, and do not eat or drink for three days, night or day. I and my young women will also fast as you do. Then I will go to the king, though it is against the law, and if I perish, I perish." Mordecai then went away and did everything as Esther had ordered him (Esther 4:15–17).

The orders Esther gave included a three day fast. I think we often consider fasting a way to petition God to do what we want, but that is not the reason for fasting. Many times in the Bible the people of God were called to fast when they faced grave situations. A story in 2 Chronicles describes King Jehoshaphat and the people seeking God by fasting. Seeking God often meant to worship Him and experience His presence. The people did not fast only to petition for help, but they fasted to receive wisdom and knowledge from the Lord concerning the situation.

> "Alarmed, Jehoshaphat resolved to inquire of the LORD,

*and he proclaimed a fast for all Judah. The people of Judah came together to seek help from the L*ord*; indeed, they came from every town in Judah to seek him. ...'Our God, will you not judge them? For we have no power to face this vast army that is attacking us. We do not know what to do, but our eyes are on you.' All the men of Judah, with their wives and children and little ones, stood before the L*ord*. Then the Spirit of the Lord came on Jahaziel the son of Zechariah, son of Benaiah, son of Jeiel, son of Mattaniah, a Levite and descendant of Asaph, as he stood in the assembly. He said, 'Listen, King Jehoshaphat and all who live in Judah and Jerusalem! This is what the L*ord* says to you: "Do not be afraid or discouraged because of this vast army. For the battle is not yours, but God's"'"* (2 Chronicles 20:3–4, 12–15 NIV).

I love everything about that passage. It is so powerful. They fasted and prayed to seek God's counsel and assistance. Fasting doesn't change God's mind. It opens our hearts and minds to better hear His voice and know how to fight. It makes way for our awareness of Him. I have to show you the rest of the story. It gets better.

*"Then Jehoshaphat bowed his head with his face to the ground, and all Judah and the inhabitants of Jerusalem fell down before the L*ord*, worshiping the L*ord*. And the Levites, of the Kohathites and the Korahites, stood up to praise the L*ord*, the God of Israel, with a very loud voice. And they rose early in the morning and went out into the wilderness of Tekoa. And when they went out, Jehoshaphat stood and said, 'Hear me, Judah and inhabitants of Jerusalem! Believe in the L*ord* your God, and you will be established; believe his prophets, and you will succeed.' And when he had taken counsel with the people, he appointed those who were to sing to the L*ord* and praise him in holy attire, as they went before the army, and say,*

'Give thanks to the LORD, for his steadfast love endures forever.'

And when they began to sing and praise, the LORD set an ambush against the men of Ammon, Moab, and Mount Seir, who had come against Judah, so that they were routed" (2 Chronicles 20:18–22).

Oh my goodness, do you have chill bumps too? I've never thought of fasting as a method of worship, but it definitely played a role in the worship of God in this story, and it culminated in God's victory. The battle belonged to the Lord, and all they had to do was believe and sing songs of thanksgiving about God's steadfast love.

By the way, "steadfast love" is really chesed (khes-ed)—His merciful covenant of acts of loving-kindness.

What did Jehoshaphat tell the people they must do? (v.20)

Believe ['Aman] in the LORD your God, and you will be established; believe his prophets, and you will succeed (addition mine).

Believe.

I believe with my mind, but this Hebrew word implies so much more. Circle the word "trust" in this definition and any words that jump out to you. Does it change the way you read Jehoshaphat's command?

💡 WORD STUDY 2

BELIEVE - Hebrew Strong's Number H539

אָמַן '**âman**, *aw-man'; a primitive root; (Isaiah 30:21; interchangeable with H541, to go to the right hand) properly, to build up or support; to foster as a parent or nurse; figuratively to render (or be) firm or faithful, to trust or believe, to be permanent or quiet; morally to be true or certain;:—hence, assurance, believe, bring up, establish, fail, be faithful (of long continuance, steadfast, sure, surely, trusty, verified), nurse, (-ing father), (put), trust, turn to the right.*

"Believe in the LORD your God, and you will be established; believe his prophets, and you will succeed."

Rewrite this verse with the words that spoke to you in the definition.

✒ JOURNAL

We've taken a rabbit trail today starting with Esther's brave decision, fasting, and faith. Close your eyes and take a deep breath in and blow it out slowly. Spend some time simply waiting on God. Write down what you hear or feel.

✋ HOLD HIS HAND

"Dear God, strengthen my faith. May my mind always go to you first when I'm afraid and in dangerous circumstances. Rather than trying to figure it out on my own help me stop and seek you and 'Aman (aw-man'). Thank you, Lord, Amen."

☕ QUESTION FOR GROUP DISCUSSION

Have you fasted before? Share your story.

DAY 2

GETTING DRESSED

I want to go shopping today. School starts in two weeks, and I really want some new clothes to start the year. Outfits can make us feel pretty or not-so-pretty. They can give us confidence—at least that's my experience. I have a feeling I'm not alone. I believe what Esther wore when she dared to stand before the king affected her too.

Another woman in the Bible put on her best, dabbed on some lipstick, and spritzed a squirt of perfume. She had some proposing to do. Her actions were also risky, and she did them out of obedience just like Esther. I love her story. In fact, I wrote a Bible study on her. She is Ruth.

One day Ruth's mother-in-law, Naomi, said to her,

> *"My daughter, I must find a home for you, where you will be well provided for. Now Boaz, with whose women you have worked, is a relative of ours. Tonight he will be winnowing barley on the threshing floor. Wash, put on perfume, and get dressed in your best clothes. Then go down to the threshing floor, but don't let him know you are there until he has finished eating and drinking. When he lies down, note the place where he is lying. Then go and uncover his feet and lie down. He will tell you what to do" (Ruth 3:1–5 NIV).*

This makes me really nervous. Maybe even more nervous than Esther. I'm not sure why. Maybe it's because it's dark. I don't know. It's just a little sketchy. Here's a little bit of what I wrote in my study:

> *"Naomi planned for Boaz to be fully satisfied, perhaps a little tipsy, and sleepy when Ruth stepped out of the shadows. She smelled good. Clean. Dressed pretty. Her appearance would reveal her purpose. She wore no work clothes that night. Ruth*

dressed for a date though Boaz was clueless."[1]

If you've read Ruth's story, you know Boaz was very kind and gracious. Her kinsman-redeemer vowed to help her, though he had to do so according to the law and another kinsman stood in line. But I don't want to get side-tracked with Ruth, let's study what happened when Esther stood before the king unannounced. One thing is for sure: she wore the right outfit.

DAILY READING

Read Esther 5:1–2.

What did Esther put on and how did the king react to her?

Read the King James Version:

> *"Now it came to pass on the third day that Esther put on her royal apparel and stood in the inner court of the king's house over against the king's house; and the king sat upon his royal throne in the royal house, over against the gate of the house. And it was so that when the king saw Esther the queen standing in the court, that she obtained favour in his sight…" (Esther 5:1–2 KJV).*

Where did Esther stand according to the KJV?

She stood in the inner court, in her royal robe, and she found favor with the king. Do you think she would've found favor with the king if she wore her old, ordinary clothes?

I see so much symbolism in this part of the story. Maybe you see it too, but if you don't, hopefully the next few scriptures will reveal what I see.

Read Hebrews 9:11, 12. What did Christ enter?

Wear your Kingdom robe today. This robe came out of God's closet. It doesn't need to be ironed. In this robe you have purpose beyond today's earthly to-do list. In this robe you are holy and set apart for special service.

💡 WORD STUDY

The ESV calls where Christ entered the "holy places." The Greek word translated is hágion (hag'-ee-on).

HOLY PLACE - Hebrew Strong's Number G39

> ἅγιον **hágion**, *hag'-ee-on; neuter of G40; a sacred thing (i.e. spot):—holiest (of all), holy place, sanctuary.*

This was a sacred part of the Temple only the high priest could enter. It was where God's Presence resided.

Read Galatians 3:27 and write down what those who've trusted Jesus "put on." Also read Isaiah 61:10 and write down what God wraps us in.

Are you starting to see the similarities? Think about what Esther put on before she went to the king, where she entered, and what she received from him. Read through Esther 5:1–2 again.

Read Hebrews 4:14–16 and write down the wonderful promise these verses proclaim in your own words. Is the throne you picture when you pray one of grace or judgment? Do you struggle with this scripture or feel loved and blessed by it?

Let's come back to Esther. Before this dire situation, I don't think Esther lived her life as the queen, at least not in her mind. I think she considered herself very ordinary. An ordinary girl chosen by a king to live in his palace. But Mordecai reminded her she had been placed in a malkûwth (mal-kooth') or royal position by God for a purpose. In this lesson we see Esther put on her royal robe, and step into the power and purpose of her position. She was no longer ordinary.

What she did represents what we must do. We who trust in Jesus have been clothed in royal robes. We have been given an invitation into the inner throne room of heaven, and there we are extended grace, favor, and mercy, but how many of us live from this place of spiritual favor? How many of us get up every day wearing our ordinary clothes rather than our "robes of righteousness" and "garments of salvation?" It's hard to imagine. We feel so ordinary and sometimes so helpless down here on this planet. But we can't rely on our feelings, we must stand on the word of God.

"But you are a chosen people, a royal priesthood, a holy nation, God's special possession, that you may declare the praises of him who called you out of darkness into his wonderful light" (1 Peter 2:9, NIV).

JOURNAL

Close your eyes for a minute and envision yourself putting on your royal robe. Is it glittery? What color is it? How does it feel? Now picture yourself walking into the throne room and God extending His scepter of grace and mercy. He asks, "What can I do for you?" Write down what you see and your petition.

HOLD HIS HAND

"Dear God, thank you for Jesus. It is so hard to comprehend that His death has not only given us life, but a malkûwth (mal-kooth'), a royal position, that allows us to enter your throne of grace. Help us put our robes on every day and use this grace to bring others to the kingdom with our prayers. Empower us to realize that we are here at this time in this position of grace for such a time as this. Amen."

QUESTION FOR GROUP DISCUSSION

Today is probably one of my favorite lessons, and yet it's also the hardest. Rather than discussing a question, spend some time in prayer together. Pray specifically for those who struggle with putting on her royal robe.

DAY 3
FIGHT

I knew this would be difficult. When the Lord said, "Five, five, five," I knew that writing a short study would be a challenge. Esther isn't a super short book. There's a lot going on and much to glean from this story. My original (unpublished) version of this study contained over 400 questions. This one has 125. Some of you just gave a sigh of relief that this version is much shorter, and a few of you Bible geeks out there want my long version.

I don't think of myself as a detail girl. I usually find details tedious, and I don't have patience for tedious. However, I love details in Scripture, and I don't want to miss one single letter. So, as I write the last three days of this study, I'm struggling because there's still so much to cover that will not be attended to.

I hope you don't see this as a cop-out, but whatever I do not include, I pray you'll go back and do your own digging. There are always a million things to learn from a book in the Bible, and there are so many delicious truths in Esther. But our focus in this study is influence, precisely Esther's influence in the place God positioned her and your influence in your piece of your world. I've had to come back to this time and time again to keep from going on too many tangents. So, I'm going to summarize what we're jumping over to get to the heart of our focus for this particular study.

But before I do, can I just speak grace over you, especially those who struggle with perfection? It's really okay if you don't cover everything. If you miss something, or you don't have time to do a study or read a book someone gave you as a gift, it's okay. Live out of the place of God's graceful leading. Let His Holy Spirit empower your choices. I believe that's what Esther did. She fasted and prayed, asked others to cover her in prayer, and after she'd prepared to go

> Live out of the place of God's graceful leading. Let His Holy Spirit empower your choices.

to the king, she did so with wisdom.

I've always been impressed with Esther's strategy. In my haste and fear, I might have blurted out my desperate plea to the king to save my people, but Esther's actions show a calculated response. She knew the king's weakness. Remember, feasts and parties were his thing. But she also wisely invited the enemy to dinner too, and the rest was history. Haman got what he deserved, and so did Mordecai. Evil never wins. Let me say that again. Evil never wins.

Ironically, Haman was hung on the gallows he built for Mordecai. Goodness prevailed. Faith and trust in God was their saving grace. Neither Mordecai nor Esther let fear get the best of them. They persevered. Somebody needs to hear that today. Don't give up.

I know I've jumped over three huge chapters, but I must stay true to my purpose. Flip on over to chapter nine. I want you to be encouraged to persevere too.

DAILY READING

Read Esther 9:1. What happened on this day?

I need to include here (because we fast forwarded through a lot) that King A. gave Esther and Mordecai the power to write a new decree because the old one could not be revoked. This edict gave the Jews permission to defend themselves against those trying to kill them (Esther 8:10–13).

According to 9:2–3, why could no one stand against the Jews and the people who helped them?

How many men were killed in Susa, and whose sons were killed? (Esther 9:6–10)

The death of Haman's sons was significant:

> *"The killing of Haman's sons is one more way that Haman's glory is diminished. It also brings his line to an end; no future threat to the Jews will come from him. Amalek is wiped out."[2]*

Also, the number of deaths (75,000 mentioned in vs 16) seems exaggerated to many scholars, but there might be an answer to such a large number. Here's commentary from Shepherds Notes:

> *"The Hebrew word translated as 'thousand' also can mean 'clan.' If the slain enemies numbered seventy-five clans their total would have been around 3,800. Regardless of the actual figure, God preserved His people in a great deliverance."[3]*

Go back to Esther 8:10, 11. What were the Jews allowed to do? Did they take any plunder?

Taking no plunder proved their integrity and reason for fighting. They simply were defending their families. I don't want us to miss the point that the Jews were not killing out of revenge but rather defense. I think this is significant. Time and time again Scripture instructs not to take revenge. But it does not tell us that we can't defend ourselves.

According to Romans 12:19, who will avenge His people?

Jesus was not a pacifist. He was a fighter, but He knew His enemy was not flesh and blood. Rather than fighting Pilate or the Jewish Council, Jesus fought for us on the cross.

Revenge is for the Lord, but we must do our part to defend ourselves and our families. That may sound contradictory to the New Testament teachings, but if you go back and study the scriptures closely, they all have to do with revenge, not defense.

One scripture that's been misunderstood and mistranslated in this context is Matthew 5:39. Most translations read: "But I say to you, Do not *resist* the one who is evil. But if anyone slaps you on the right cheek, turn to him the other also" (emphasis mine). However, the Good News Translations writes it this way:

"But now I tell you: do not take *revenge* on someone who wrongs you. If anyone slaps you on the right cheek, let him slap your left cheek too" (emphasis mine).

WORD STUDY

In this case, the study of the Greek word does mean "resist." Simply looking at the definition is not enough. Context is needed. It's going to take a little extra time today to do this, but I'm compelled by the importance to reveal this misunderstanding. It is crucial concerning our position and purpose. Take a deep breath and pray for revelation here.

Context: Matthew 5:38–39 (My ESV entitles this section "Retaliation.")

> *"You have heard that it was said, 'Eye for eye, and tooth for tooth.' But I tell you, do not resist an evil person. If anyone slaps you on the right cheek, turn to them the other cheek also."*

"An eye for an eye" and "a tooth for a tooth" refer to revenge. David Bivin, who wrote *New Light on the Difficult Words of Jesus: Insights from His Jewish Context*, explains Jesus' words this way:

> *"In idiomatic English, Matthew 5:39a might read simply, 'Don't try to get even with evil doers.' Not 'competing' with evil doers is*

very different from not resisting evildoers. Jesus was not teaching that one should submit to evil, but that one should not seek revenge…English mistranslation of Matthew 5:39a has created a theological contradiction, but when Jesus' saying is correctly understood, it harmonizes beautifully with other New Testament passages." [4]

One of these passages is from Paul:

"See that no one repays anyone evil for evil; but always seek to do good to one another and to everyone" (1 Thessalonians 5:15).

If you've struggled with discrepancies between the Old Testament and the New, that is invitation to study. Always connect the two. I'm convinced that if there is contradiction, it is because we've missed something somewhere. Jesus was not a pacifist. He was a fighter, but He knew His enemy was not flesh and blood. Rather than fighting Pilate or the Jewish Council, Jesus fought for us on the cross.

Choose your battles wisely. Never let them be for revenge.

Let's get back to Esther, back to that battle. Why was it good that Haman's edict (for the Jews destruction) could not be revoked? What would have eventually happened if the Jews did not have the opportunity to kill the people who hated them?

JOURNAL

Have you asked God to make something easier, but He didn't or hasn't? Could there be a good reason for the struggle?

HOLD HIS HAND

"Dear Father, I know you are good. I know you've won the war. Yet, battles still must be fought. Strengthen my faith and resolve. Make me a warrior for my family, for those I love. Don't let me give up the fight. Amen."

QUESTION FOR GROUP DISCUSSION

How can we apply the truth of this lesson to our lives? What battles do you need to fight?

DAY 4

FOR GENERATIONS TO COME

The greatest legacy one can pass on to one's children and grandchildren is not money or other material things accumulated in one's life, but rather a legacy of character and faith.
—Billy Graham

At the end of their time in the concentration camp, Corrie's sister Betsie, grew very ill. The last few days, between fits of coughing and fever, Betsie told Corrie of visions of the ministry ahead. It seemed all would be well, and they would both survive the horror they were living. Yet one morning Betsie could not walk. She was too weak to move, and she was taken to the infirmary. Corrie wrote:

Sleet stung us as we reached the outside. I stepped close to the stretcher to form a shield for Betsie. We walked past the waiting line of sick people, through the door and into the large ward. They placed the stretcher on the floor, and I leaned down to make out Betsie's words.

" …must tell people what we have learned here. We must tell them that there is no pit so deep that He is deeper still. They will listen to us, Corrie, because we have been here."

I stared at her wasted form. "But when will this happen, Betsie!"

"Now, right away. Oh, very soon! By the first of the year, Corrie, we will be out of prison!"[5]

Betsie's prediction came to pass. They were both freed, though not as they had hoped. Betsie's spirit slipped away through heaven's gates, and a few days later Corrie found herself walking through the gates of Ravensbruk a free woman. She would learn later that her freedom was a clerical error. God Himself had set them both free.

Corrie experienced the reality of every vision Betsie had shared, and she faithfully proclaimed the love, truth, and healing power of Jesus all over the world. It was true, her testimony bore the weight of one who'd lived everything she taught. She'd faced the darkness of evil, the shadows of hopelessness, and the faithfulness of an invisible God. Would her ministry have impacted the world without the testimony that accompanied it? No.

She wore no crown as Esther did. She wrote a book rather than an edict to be followed. But Corrie Ten-Boom's life impacted mine. And that, my friends, is what our radiant influence is all about. Other people.

DAILY READING

Read Esther 9:20–22. What were they specifically commemorating, and how were the Jews to celebrate Purim according to Mordecai's letter?

Why would they give gifts to the poor to celebrate this holiday?

Read Esther 9:26–29. Why did the Jews agree to the "obligation" of celebrating Purim for generations to come?

What did Queen Esther do after Mordecai sent his letters out? (Esther 9:29–32). Why would she do this?

This time the queen's "signet ring" sealed the fate of the Jewish people to memorialize the day that God saved them. Esther had stepped into her identity as queen, and she would continue to walk in that authority and position. Esther was solidifying this edict to remember what God had done. Her letter confirmed Mordecai's decree. But her letters had significance beyond the Persian kingdom.

Esther's letter authorized this holiday not only for the Jews in Persia living in that day and time, but she ordained this feast to memorialize the salvation of God's people for generations to come. If this isn't a girl-power book of the Bible I don't know what is. Yet we must not forget Mordecai and the role he played. This is a Kingdom of God book where both men and women play important roles.

Read Esther 10:1–3. At what rank was Mordecai placed? Why was Mordecai great among the Jews and popular with the multitudes? (Esther 10:3)

> This is a Kingdom of God book where both men and women play important roles.

"…for he sought the welfare of his people and spoke peace to all his people."

Let's do some digging.

💡 WORD STUDY

WEALTH - Hebrew Strong's Number H2896

בוֹט **ṭôwb**, tobe; from H2895; good (as an adjective) in the widest sense; used likewise as a noun, both in the masculine and the feminine, the singular and the plural (good, a good or good thing, a good man or woman; the good, goods or good things, good men or women), also as an adverb (well):—beautiful, best, better, bountiful, cheerful, at ease, × fair (word), (be in) favour, fine, glad, good (deed, -lier, -liest, -ly, -ness, -s), graciously, joyful, kindly, kindness, liketh (best), loving, merry, × most, pleasant, pleaseth, pleasure, precious, prosperity, ready, sweet, wealth, welfare, (be) well(-favoured).

PEACE - Hebrew Strong's Number H7965

םוֹלשָׁ **shâlôwm**, shaw-lome'; or םלֹשָׁ shâlôm; from H7999; safe, i.e. (figuratively) well, happy, friendly; also (abstractly) welfare, i.e. health, prosperity, peace:—× do, familiar, × fare, favour, friend, × great, (good) health, (× perfect, such as be at) peace(-able, -ably), prosper(-ity, -ous), rest, safe(-ty), salute, welfare, (× all is, be) well, × wholly.

Mordecai sought the good of his people and spoke peace to everyone. Haman was always focused on himself, but Mordecai cared about others. His efforts were always toward helping his people. And that's the end of the story…at least in the book of Esther, but it's not the end of THE STORY. We'll conclude tomorrow with that, but let's linger a little longer together today to unpack what we can glean from the end of Esther and the legacy she left.

✎ JOURNAL

Where did Esther and Mordecai find their strength and hope? Write down some things you could do to develop such strength. To whom do you hope to leave a legacy of faith?

✋ HOLD HIS HAND

"Dear Father, I want my life to leave a legacy. I want to glorify you in my words, actions, and faith. Holy Spirit, lead me, speak through me, make me bold yet gentle and kind. May I bring shâlôwm (shaw-lome') wherever I go. Amen."

> *"But the fruit of the Spirit is love, joy, peace, patience, kindness, goodness, faithfulness, gentleness, and self-control. Against such things there is no law" (Galatians 5:22–23).*

☕ QUESTION FOR GROUP DISCUSSION

Who has been a radiant influence in your life? What was it about them? What is their legacy?

DAY 5

IDENTITY

When we think of the story of Esther we think of her bravery and wisdom. She was a beautiful heroin who won the day with the help of her adoptive father, Mordecai. It's a perfect Disney movie. But what really strikes me in this story after digging deep and reading it over and over is not Esther's bravery or beauty or Mordecai's tenacity, but their trust in their God—the God of their people. The God of the Jews. Though it's as if He is missing in this book—His name never mentioned—He is so very much there. I'm struck by their great sense of identity and undeniable faith in God's hand in their life.

Esther and Mordecai were not entitled.

There was no sign of anger with God when life got hard.

They simply trusted His goodness and His love for His people.

They fasted and prayed. Repented in sack cloth and ashes and waited for Him to save them.

And He did.

And just as God saved the Jews in Esther's story, He is still with them today. The Jews will one day be saved. If you read any of my books, you know that this is a message I feel is part of my legacy. I don't ever want to miss a chance to try to re-teach what I once learned incorrectly growing up in the church.

I was wrongly taught that the Christian church has replaced the Jews. We did not replace them; we were grafted into their family. The Jews have suffered genocide, hatred, and radical racism all through their existence, but God has not forgotten them. As we close this study, it's so important to know who our family is—it's another facet to our identity and purpose. Esther is our sister, too.

⟿ DAILY READING

Read Romans 11:25–27. Why has God allowed a partial hardening of Israel? How much of Israel will be saved?

Read Romans 11:28–29. Why are the Jews loved by God, and what does Romans 11:29 say about God's gifts and His call?

If God's gifts and His call cannot be revoked, how does this apply to us, also children of God, chosen by Him and called?

His chesed is relentless. Once He has made a covenant with us, it cannot be broken. His promise to the Israelites, and His unrelenting favor and love for them should give us an extra boost of confidence in our God.

And then there is Jesus.

Read Romans 8:1. What does it promise? And what has set us free from the law of sin and death? (v.2)

Read Romans 8:14–17. What Spirit have we received? If we are adopted children, what does that make us? (v. 17)

"For those who are led by the Spirit of God are the children of God. The Spirit you received does not make you slaves, so that you live in fear again; rather, the Spirit you received brought about your adoption to sonship. And by him we cry, 'Abba, Father.' The Spirit himself testifies with our spirit that we are God's children. Now if we are children, then we are heirs—heirs of God and co-heirs with Christ, if indeed we share in his sufferings in order that we may also share in his glory" (NIV).

My goal for this study was for us to find identity and purpose. The truth is those two things are not found in one day or one Bible study. Identity and purpose are found day by day. They are a process. A journey. Our identity in Christ as beloved daughters of God and heirs with Jesus comes by faith and faith alone. That faith is strengthened and deepened by studying the Bible and letting it "get in you." Faith comes by trusting His goodness even in the hard things, and it comes by memorializing all the faithful and good things God has done for us.

✎ JOURNAL

Identity: Has there been a time in your life when God saved you? Have you told Him you want Him to be your God? Have you told Jesus you want Him to be your King? If you haven't, write a prayer of surrender. A prayer of trust. A prayer of love. If you have already done those things, write down your memory. And celebrate. Mark it on the calendar and celebrate your Purim, the day God saved you.

Purpose: I believe purpose comes in all shapes and sizes and that God has many purposes for His girls. He has purpose for us right where we are. Think eternal. Think blessing others. Why would God have you in the place you are today?

"And who knows whether you have come to the kingdom for such a time as this."

A poem for you…

Whose You Are

I must tell you to put on your royal robe.
I must remind you of whose you are.
Not who you are.
Or who you think you should be.
Or who you want to be.
But.
Whose you are.
You are a child of God.
The God-creator of the universe.
The One who loves you so much He sacrificed His Son for you.
You are chosen by Him to be in His family.
He chose you before you chose Him.
You belong to the firstborn.
That means you are of those who will receive the inheritance of the Father.
The heavenly kingdom that cannot be shaken.
You belong to the King of kings.
The Lord of lords.
Who is Good.
Kind.
Faithful.
Even when we are faithless.
He is holy.
He is merciful loving-kindness.
Holy chesed.
He gives peace.
Not as the world gives.
He expects nothing in return.
But we can't receive that peace if we don't trust the goodness…
Of whose we are.
Trust Him.
And experience victory.
Fight mighty warrior.

Fight.
Be a woman
Of radiant influence
And help save your world.

🖐 HOLD HIS HAND

"Dear God, give me the faith of Esther and Mordecai, their trust in Your power and faithfulness. Grant me the assurance they had as children of God. They never doubted who they were in You. Help me rise to the positions and purposes You've placed me in Jesus. I'm putting on my royal robe of righteousness. You are ṭôwb (tobe). Your chesed (kheh'-sed) endures forever. Hallelujah! Amen."

☕ QUESTION FOR GROUP DISCUSSION

What have you learned these past five weeks that will affect the way you live?

I hate saying goodbye...

Thank you for joining me in this study of Esther. I pray that the scripture came to life and even if you've studied this book a hundred times before, you gleaned fresh insights. Most of all I pray that your faith roots have grown deeper and stronger.

Never doubt how important you are, the radiant influence you have in your world.

WEEK FIVE VIDEO NOTES

Finally

FINALLY

If you enjoyed this study, there are a few things you can do to help others know about it and open doors for the publication of other Bible studies and books. Here's what you can do:

Write a review on Amazon.

Share a social media post about the study.

Recommend it to other women's ministry groups and your friends.

Invite me to speak at your next event. (I would love to meet you!)

Pray for this ministry.

I'm honored that you chose *Radiant Influence*. And I loved spending these five weeks with you. Connect with me on my website, wordsbyandylee.com, and social media outlets, and subscribe to www.youtube.com/c/andyleebible on YouTube for encouraging messages and more Bible study. That way, we don't have to say goodbye.

Breathe deep.

Let it out slowly.

Go influence the world for Jesus.

LEADER'S GUIDE & PURIM PARTIES

I'm so thankful for your willingness to facilitate this study. Here are a few suggestions to help the meetings go smoother. Through the years I've learned a lot about leading Bible studies, and as I wrote *Radiant Influence*, I kept these thoughts in mind.

5 GROUP QUESTIONS

I wrote questions specifically for group discussion. As a leader, I've often struggled choosing which questions from a study to use during the small group. I've experienced it's impossible to answer all the questions of a study and watch a video. Let's face it, your time is limited especially if childcare is involved. Your group is filled with busy women. With five questions allocated for your time together, everyone has more time to share. Of course, if you feel led to discuss some of the other questions, please do. Let the Holy Spirit lead your leading.

5 PARTICIPANTS

One of my dear friends suggested to invite only five women to your small group. Five is the number the Lord gave me for this series, so I think she may be onto something. Do you have a friend who hears from God so powerfully that you know you should do what she says? Well, that's my friend, Debbie. So, consider keeping your group to five, or if you have a large group, break into groups of five to discuss the questions and then come together for the video.

START WITH WORSHIP

I am not a worship leader. The only solos I do are silent (sign language worship.) But you don't have to be a beautiful singer to lead worship. I encourage you to find a worshipful song to play at the beginning of your meetings. It's important to spend some time worshipping the Lord and setting aside all the worries and business of the day before jumping into the Word.

PRAYER CARDS

Though it's great to open up time to share prayer needs this can take a lot of time from your study. A great prayer tactic is to give everyone an index card to write a prayer request on. Encourage them to sign their card so the person praying for them knows whom they are praying for. It's really awesome to have these cards throughout the week to be praying for each other. Place the cards in a pile and have each woman take one home to pray through during the week.

WATCH THE VIDEO AFTER DISCUSSION

The videos provide extra information regarding the week you've discussed, and they introduce the heart matters for the following week. They are 15-20 minutes in length. Pages for notes can be found in your study to be used during the videos. Encourage your ladies to take notes for further group discussion.

PURIM PARTIES

I hope you'll consider having a Purim Party after you've finished the five weeks. If you make the first week an introduction week and then have the Purim party after the five weeks of the study, you will be together seven weeks total, two being fellowship gatherings. That is important. I pray these parties will not only be another learning opportunity, but I hope they will be filled with laughter and some silliness. Let's face it: we are all guilty of taking ourselves way too seriously. I pray you will simply have fun.

Traditionally, Purim parties are costume parties. You can dress up like characters in Esther's story, or you may give your Purim party a theme like a western Purim or a Purim Luau. The sky is the limit. I can't wait to hear about your creativity and see your pictures! If you follow me on Instagram @wordsbyandylee, tag me on your Purim Party photos and use the hashtag #radiantstudy.

At the end of this guide, you will find a traditional and nontraditional recipe for your Purim celebration and games to play provided by Debbie, my game-playing, God-hearing sister.

GIFTS TO THE POOR

Finally, Purim is a time to give food to those in need. Mordecai declared that Purim was a time " …of feasting and gladness and of sending food to one another, as well as gifts to the poor." Pray with your group about to whom you want to give your Purim gifts. At the end of your time together make a basket of food or other necessities to give away. This is known as tzedakah (seh·duh·kuh). The word means "righteousness," but it is used to signify charity.

ICEBREAKER, GAMES, AND RECIPES

Give-and-Take-Away (Icebreaker for the first or second meeting)

We did this icebreaker at one of our women's retreats, and it was powerful.

Choose something positive that begins with the first letter of your name. This is something you want to give to the group during your study of *Radiant Influence*. Also choose something negative beginning with the first letter of your name that you want to take away from the group. Each lady repeats the names of those before her and the give-and-take-aways.

For example:

First person: Andy says, "My name is Andy, and I want to give amazing grace (I cheated a little) and take away anxiety."

Second person: Stacey says, "Her name is Andy, and she wants to give amazing grace and take away anxiety. My name is Stacy, and I want to give singing and take away sorrow."

Third Person: Haley says, "Andy wants to give amazing grace and take away anxiety. Stacey wants to give singing and take away sorrow. I'm Haley, and I want to give healing and take away heaviness."

After each lady has shared, spend some time in prayer together praying over the give-and-take-aways spoken.

Games for the Purim Party

Musical Ball

Use a ball to pass like musical chairs. When the music stops the person with the ball answers one of these questions:

1. What person do you most relate to in Esther's story? Explain.
2. What did you glean the most from the study?
3. What's the part of Esther's story you struggle with the most?

Costume Party Contest

Vote for the best costume with secret ballots. Make a silly crown for the winner.

Who Am I? (Three Versions)

1. Sticky-note version - Write the names of famous biblical people on sticky notes. Each participant takes turns in the "hot seat." During her turn, the host puts the sticky note on the participants forehead, and she has two minutes to ask questions to help her guess who she is. Have one of the members use the stopwatch on her phone to time the questions.

2. Charade's version - Each person is given a name and must act out the biblical character they were given.

3. Pictionary version - Each person must draw the biblical character they were given.

Easy Purim Recipes

I am not a baker. I will bake, and I do bake during the holidays or for birthdays because my momma and mamaw always baked for us. It was their love language. I know it's a lovely love language and some of you reading are bakers and might be offended if I don't give you a traditional recipe for the Purim cookies called hamantaschen (haa·muhn·taa·shn). With my very good friend Marybeth in mind, who calls me a half-baker, I will give you a traditional recipe. I'm also, however, sharing an Andy Lee quick and easy "knock-off" hamantaschen (haa·muhn·taa·shn) recipe I recently invented for this book. It has been tested and tried. I have no doubt they are not as yummy as the traditional recipe, but they look the part! I have not attempted the traditional recipe, but I know someone who has.

The name for these treats has different meanings. Some say they mean Haman's pockets, others say they represent his hat, and others believe they represent his ears. The ear theory has something to do with his ears being cut off before he was hung on the gallows. I know, I kind of like the hat or pockets theory better. Whether you are a hat, pockets, or ears gal, a traditional baker or one that goes for the easy-peasy recipe, I hope you have a blast making hamantaschen.

Ingredients for the dough:

½ cup butter, softened
¼ cup of light or dark brown sugar
¼ cup of honey
2 large eggs
1 tsp vanilla
½ tsp of baking soda
1 tsp of baking powder
2 ½ cups flour

For the dough, use an electric mixer at medium speed to cream the butter with the brown sugar and honey in a medium sized bowl until light and fluffy. Beat in the eggs and vanilla. Then mix the baking powder, soda, and flour until very well combined. Form the dough into a thick circle, wrap it in plastic wrap or wax paper, and refrigerate for several hours or until it is quite firm. (The dough may be made ahead and refrigerated up to three days.)

Roll out chilled dough on a lightly floured surface until it is about 1/8 inch thick. (For easier handling, use half the dough at a time and the rest in the refrigerator.) Cut out circles about 3 inches in diameter.[1]

This recipe included a poppy seed filling made from scratch; this is, however, a busy woman study, so please make this as simple or work intensive as you want. Hamantaschen is filled with sweet or savory deliciousness. Jams are great to use or flavorful cheese spreads. My easy recipe on the next page describes how to fold and bake the hamantaschen.

Andy Lee's Easy Hamantaschen

Ingredients

1 package of prepared, ready to bake pie crust. (Two rolls come in a package.)
Your favorite jam.
Granulated or decorative sugar or powdered sugar

Directions

1. Line cookie sheet with parchment paper and preheat oven according to the baking directions on the pastry box.
2. Unroll pastry according to the box's directions. Using a 3-inch cookie cutter or small cup 3 inches in diameter, cut out circles and place on cookie sheet.
3. Sprinkle the pastry with granulated sugar.
4. Place a tablespoon of jam in the center of the pastry circles.
5. Fold the tops of each circle to a point then fold the bottom to the center forming a triangle. Pinch the corners.
6. Sprinkle with sugar if desired. You may use colored, decorative sugar.
7. Bake according to the pastry directions.
8. Sprinkle with powdered sugar once cooled.

Other Foods Eaten During Purim

Chickpeas! The tradition for making recipes with chickpeas and beans goes back to Esther's Jewish heritage and her fast. Just as Daniel would not eat the rich foods of the Babylonian king, tradition teaches that Esther refrained also. We do know she fasted for three days and nights, but perhaps she also fasted from the rich foods of the Persian court. So…bring on the hummus and all things chickpeas, bean, and lentil related.

Two of my go-to websites for Jewish foods and holidays are: Chabad.org and My Jewish-learning.org. I hope you'll check these out.

ENDNOTES

WEEK ONE

1. Kisha Gallagher, "Hebrew Numbers 1-10," Grace in Torah, June 15, 2015, https://gracein-torah.net/2015/06/15/hebrew-numbers-1-10/.

2. Walter C. Kaiser, Jr and Duane Garrett, eds., *NIV Archeological Study Bible: An Illustrated Walk through Biblical History and Culture*, (Grand Rapids: Zondervan, 2005), 730.

3. John J. Parsons. "Purim, Feast of Lots," Hebrew for Christians, access date June 10, 2020, http://www.hebrew4christians.com/Holidays/Winter_Holidays/Purim/purim.html.

4. Corrie Ten Boom, John and Elizabeth Sherrill, *The Hiding Place*, (New York: Bantam Books, 1971), 201.

5. David Guzik, "Esther 2—Esther is Chosen Queen,"Enduring Word, access date June 8, 2020, https://enduringword.com/bible-commentary/esther-2/.

6. Corrie Ten Boom, John and Elizabeth Sherrill, *The Hiding Place*, (New York: Bantam Books, 1971), 196.

7. Adele Berlin and Mark Zvi Brettler, eds. The Jewish Study Bible, (New York: Oxford University Press, 2004), 1628.

8. Annesley William Streane, "Commentary on Esther," *Cambridge Bible for Schools and Colleges Commentary*, (Cambridge, MA: Cambridge University Press, 1907), accessed June 8, 2020, https://biblehub.com/commentaries/cambridge/esther/2.htm.

9. Robert Lintzenich, Shepherds Notes, Ruth and Esther, (Nashville: B&H Publishing Group), 1998, 46.

10. Touraj Daryaee. "History/On Iranians, Drinking Wine, and Cultural Stereotyping", Frontline, December 16, 2012, http://www.pbs.org/wgbh/pages/frontline/tehranbureau/2012/12/history-on-iranians-drinking-wine-and-cultur-al-stereotyping.html#ixzz3VENX6Yvl.

11. Elissa Blattman, "The Girl Who Acted Before Rosa Parks." National Women's History Museum, February 17, 2017. http://www.womenshistory.org/articles/girl-who-acted-rosa-parks.

12. Ibid.

13. Adele Berlin and Mark Zvi Brettler, eds. The Jewish Study Bible, (New York: Oxford University Press, 2004), 1628.

14. Brown, Fausset, Jamieson, Clarke, and Henry, *The Bethany Parallel Commentaries on the Old Testament*, (Minneapolis: Bethany House Publishers, 1985), 857.

WEEK TWO

1. Adele Berlin and Mark Zvi Brettler, eds. The Jewish Study Bible, (New York: Oxford University Press, 2004), 1627.

2. Ibid.

3. S. Michael Houdmann, "When the Bible says God remembered something, what does that mean?" Compelling Truth, January 1, 2015, https://www.compellingtruth.org/God-remembered.html.

4. "Moving Kings and Kingdoms," One for Israel, October 29, 2020, https://www.oneforisrael.org/bible-based-teaching-from-israel/moving-kings-and-kingdoms/

5. Corrie Ten Boom, John and Elizabeth Sherrill, *The Hiding Place*, (New York: Bantam Books, 1971), 143.

6. Brown, Fausset, Jamieson, Clarke, and Henry, *The Bethany Parallel Commentaries on the Old Testament*, (Minneapolis: Bethany House Publishers, 1985), 857.

WEEK THREE

1. Corrie Ten Boom, John and Elizabeth Sherrill, *The Hiding Place*, (New York: Bantam Books, 1971), 163–164.

2. Brown, Fausset, Jamieson, Clarke, and Henry, *The Bethany Parallel Commentaries on the Old Testament*, (Minneapolis: Bethany House Publishers, 1985), 857.

3. Adele Berlin and Mark Zvi Brettler, eds. The Jewish Study Bible, (New York: Oxford University Press, 2004), 1628.

4. Lois Tverberg, *Walking in the Dust of Rabbi Jesus: How the Jewish Words of Jesus Can Change Your Life*, (Grand Rapids, MI: Zondervan, 2012), 84.

5. "Megillah," Encyclopedia Britannica. Accessed August 09, 2020; Formatted: February 22, 2007, from https://www.britannica.com/topic/Megillah.

WEEK FOUR

1. Joseph Benson, *Benson Commentary of the Old and the New Testament*, (New York: T. Carlton and J. Porter, 1857), https://biblehub.com/commentaries/esther/2-18.htm.

2. Annesley William Streane, "Commentary on Esther," *Cambridge Bible for Schools and Colleges*, (Cambridge University Press, 1907), https://biblehub.com/commentaries/esther/2-18.htm.

3. Walter C. Kaiser, Jr and Duane Garrett, eds., *NIV Archeological Study Bible: An Illustrated Walk through Biblical History and Culture*, (Grand Rapids: Zondervan, 2005), 719.

4. Ibid, 721

5. David Stern, *Jewish New Testament Commentary*, (Clarksville, MD: Jewish New Testament Publications, 1992), 798.

6. Robert Lintzenich, Shepherds Notes, Ruth and Esther, (Nashville: B&H Publishing Group), 1998, 67.

7. "Ancient Jewish History: The Urim and Thummim", American-Israeli Cooperative Enterprise, accessed August 20, 2020, https://www.jewishvirtuallibrary.org/the-urim-and-thummim.

8. Martin H. Manser ed., *Dictionary of Bible Themes*, (BookBaby, 1996), https://www.biblegateway.com/resources/dictionary-of-bible-themes/6742-sackcloth-ashes

WEEK FIVE

1. Andy Lee, *The Book of Ruth Key Word Study: A 31-Day Journey to Hope and Promise*, (Chattanooga: AMG Publishers, 2015), 149.

2. Adele Berlin and Mark Zvi Brettler, eds. The Jewish Study Bible, (New York: Oxford University Press, 2004), 1637.

3. Robert Lintzenich, Shepherds Notes, Ruth and Esther, (Nashville: B&H Publishing Group, 1998), 95.

4. David Bivins, *New Light on the Difficult Words of Jesus: Insights from His Jewish Context*, (Holland, MI: En-Gedi Resource Center, 2007), 106.

5. Corrie Ten Boom, John and Elizabeth Sherrill, *The Hiding Place*, (New York: Bantam Books, 1971), 217.

LEADER'S GUIDE & PURIM PARTIES

1. Gloria Kauffer Greene, The Jewish Holiday Cookbook, (New York: Times Books, 1985), 215–216.

BIBLIOGRAPHY

Berlin, Adele and Mark Zvi Brettler, eds. The Jewish Study Bible. New York: Oxford University Press, 2004.

Bivins, David. New Light on the Difficult Words of Jesus: Insights from His Jewish Context. Holland, MI: En-Gedi Resource Center, 2007.

Blattman, Elissa. "The Girl Who Acted Before Rosa Parks". National Women's History Museum February 17, 2017. http://www.womenshistory.org/articles/girl-who-acted-rosa-parks.

Brown, Fausset, Jamieson, Clarke, and Henry. The Bethany Parallel Commentaries on the Old Testament. Minneapolis: Bethany House Publishers, 1985.

Daryaee, Tourai. "History/On Iranians, Drinking Wine, and Cultural Stereotyping". Frontline, December 16, 2012 http://www.pbs.org/wgbh/pages/frontline/tehranbureau/2012/12/history-on-iranians-drinking-wine-and-cultural-stereotyping.html#ixzz3VENX6Yvl.

Gallagher, Kisha. "Hebrew Numbers 1-10," Grace in Torah, June 15, 2015https://graceintorah.net/2015/06/15/hebrew-numbers-1-10/.

Guzik, David. "Esther 2—Esther is Chosen Queen," Enduring Word. Access date June 8, 2020. https://enduringword.com/bible-commentary/esther-2/.

Houdmann, S. Michael. "When the Bible says God remembered something, what does that mean?" Compelling Truth. January 1, 2015. https://www.compellingtruth.org/God-remembered.html.

Kaiser, Walter C. Jr and Duane Garrett, eds., NIV Archeological Study Bible: An Illustrated Walk through Biblical History and Culture. Grand Rapids: Zondervan, 2005.

Lee, Andy. The Book of Ruth Key Word Study: A 31-Day Journey to Hope and Promise. Chattanooga: AMG Publishers, 2015.

Lintzenich, Robert. Shepherds Notes, Ruth and Esther. Nashville: B&H Publishing Group, 1998.

Parsons, John J. "Purim, Feast of Lots," Hebrew for Christians, access date June 10, 2020 http://www.hebrew4christians.com/Holidays/Winter_Holidays/Purim/purim.html.

Streane, Annesley William. "Commentary on Esther". Cambridge Bible for Schools and Colleges Commentary. Cambridge, MA: Cambridge University Press, 1907. Accessed June 8, 2020. https://biblehub.com/commentaries/cambridge/esther/2.htm.

Ten Boom, C., J. Sherrill, and E. Sherrill. The Hiding Place. New York: Bantam Books, 1971.

Tverberg, Lois. Walking in the Dust of Rabbi Jesus: How the Jewish Words of Jesus Can Change Your Life. Grand Rapids, MI: Zondervan, 2012.

"Moving Kings and Kingdoms," One For Israel, October 29, 2020, https://www.oneforisrael.org/bible-based-teaching-from-israel/moving-kings-and-kingdoms/

ABOUT THE AUTHOR

When God called **Andy Lee** into ministry a hundred years ago, she had a vision. She was (23) dressed in a clergy robe, holding a Bible and standing in front of an old wooden altar. She knew it was a call to preach and pastor, but rather than shepherding adults in a steepled building, Andy has shepherded women's hearts through her books, speaking events, and just being a friend. She lives on the Carolina Coast with her retired soldier and their orange tabby, Hank, who keeps the empty nest not so empty. Her favorite things are grandbabies, peanut M&M's, the ocean, and Starbucks Carmel Crunch Frappuccinos. Connect with Andy on...

Wordsbyandylee.com
Instagram.com/wordsbyandylee
Youtube.com/c/andyleebible

Discover more great books at
CrossRiverMedia.com

UNBEATEN
Lindsey Bell

Difficult times often leave Christians searching the Bible for answers to the most difficult questions—Does God hear me when I pray? Why isn't He doing anything? Author Lindsey Bell understands the struggle. As she searched the Bible for answers to these tough questions, her studies led her through the stories of biblical figures, big and small. She discovered that while life brings trials, faith brings victory. And when we rely on God for the strength to get us through, we can emerge *Unbeaten*.

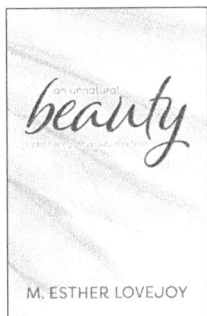

AN UNNATURAL BEAUTY
Esther Lovejoy

Holiness is not an endless list of "thou shalt nots." It's not how we behave, what we think, or how we react or respond to life and the people around us. You'll discover foundational truths from Scripture, the path to a deeper, more intimate relationship with God, and why holiness can't be achieved through our own efforts. With relatable stories, Esther reminds us that Holiness is not a what, but a glorious Who, and He's inviting you to share in His divine nature.

HANDS FULL
Brooke Ellen Frick

You know it. They know it. Everyone in the store knows it. You've got your hands full. It is the nature of life with little ones. In this humorous take on life and lessons learned living with her hands full, Brooke shares from her heart about her struggle to live out the fullness of her faith in the midst of the demands of motherhood and the redeeming love and grace available in Jesus. With His grace, we can empty these full hands into the hands of the One who holds the whole world.

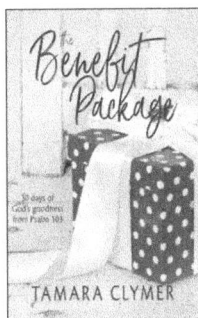

THE BENEFIT PACKAGE
Tamara Clymer

Love, redemption, mercy, provision, revelation and healing… In Psalm 103, David listed just a few of the good things God did for him. His list gives us plenty to be thankful for during tough times. No matter your circumstances or background, God is always full of compassion, generous with his mercy, unfailing in his love and powerful in healing. When circumstances overwhelm you — unwrap his *Benefit Package* and rediscover God's goodness.

The grace Impact

a devotional

How God's grace covers every aspect of our life.

More great books from
CrossRiverMedia.com

MARRIAGE CONVERSATIONS
Cathy Primer Krafve

Marriage requires serious communication. So, we turn to the Master Communicator for strategies to soften hearts and strengthen resolve. Cathy will help you initiate practical, foundational truths; replace magical thinking with rock solid miraculous biblical truths; understand why we get married in the first place; and invigorate your closest relationship. Inspire the breathtaking relationship your heart is craving.

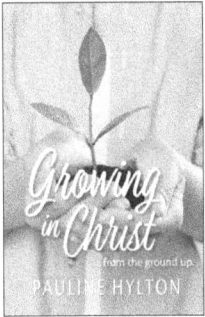

GROWING IN CHRIST
Pauline Hylton

Pauline and her husband, Tom, sold their charter fishing boat and house on a quarter acre in sunny Clearwater, Florida, to move to a sixty-six-acre tobacco farm that Tom inherited outside of Mount Airy, North Carolina. They had a dream of growing their own food. *Growing in Christ – from the ground up*, chronicles the four years Tom and Pauline have farmed in North Carolina. They have experienced a few successes but mostly failures. However, God's economy is never wasted. He wove their mid-life-change-of-life into a tapestry of His grace.

NEXT STEP
DeeDee Lake

You've accepted Jesus. Now what? Author DeeDee Lake has been where you are. A brand new Christian with no idea of what you do now? No need to feel lost. In *Next Step*, you'll discover answers for what's next for you as a brand new Christian, eye-opening "what I wish I knew as a teen" advice, letters and prayers from DeeDee for you, answers to who the Bible says you are, along with practical tips, doable action steps and weekly videos. You'll learn you aren't alone.

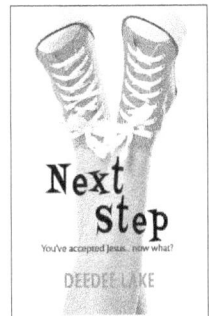

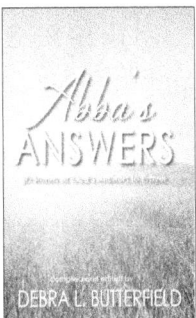

ABBA'S ANSWERS
Debra L. Butterfield

No prayer is too small or too big for God to answer. Do you feel like God couldn't possibly care about your prayers? Take heart. He cares about every detail of our lives! In *Abba's Answers*, you'll find thirty uplifting personal accounts of how God answered prayer. From being stranded in the midst of a snowstorm, to finding a lost ring, to bringing new friends, our heavenly Father is eager to answer. All you have to do is ask!

Andy Lee Live Abundantly

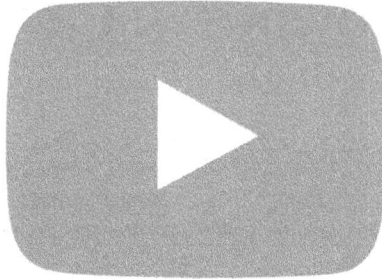

www.youtube.com/c/andyleebible.

Continue your Bible journey with Andy.

Subscribe for fresh biblical insights, timely teachings, and authentic, heartfelt messages for abundant living.

Don't forget to hit the notification bell!

If you enjoyed this book, will you consider sharing it with others?

- Please mention the book on Facebook, Twitter, Pinterest, or your blog.

- Recommend this book to your small group, book club, and workplace.

- Head over to Facebook.com/CrossRiverMedia, 'Like' the page and post a comment as to what you enjoyed the most.

- Pick up a copy for someone you know who would be challenged or encouraged by this message.

- Write a review on Amazon, Barnes and Noble, Walmart or Goodreads.

- To learn about our latest releases subscribe to our newsletter at www.CrossRiverMedia.com.

www.ingramcontent.com/pod-product-compliance
Lightning Source LLC
LaVergne TN
LVHW061305060426
835513LV00013B/1245